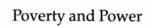

Poverty and Power

POVERTY

and

POWER

The Political
Representation of
Poor Americans

Douglas R. Imig

University of Nebraska Press
Lincoln and London

© 1996 by the University of Nebraska Press

All rights reserved

Manufactured in the United States of America

The paper in this book meets

the minimum requirements of American National

Standard for Information Sciences –

Permanence of Paper for Printed Library Materials,

ANSI Z39.48-1984.

Library of Congress Cataloging-in-Publication Data

Imig, Douglas R., 1962–

Poverty and power: the political representation of

poor Americans / Douglas R. Imig.

p.   cm.

Includes bibliographical references (p.   ) and index.

ISBN 0-8032-2500-8 (cl: alk. paper)

1. Poor—United States—Political activity.

2. Economic assistance, Domestic—United States.

3. Public welfare—United States.

4. Pressure groups—United States.

5. United States—Politics and government—1981–1989.

HC110.P6I45   1996

322.4´4´0973—dc20

95-17949   CIP

Dedicated to the memory of Elmer Wells Rowley, 1909–1988

Contents

Illustrations

Acknowledgments

This is a book about public-interest groups and social movements for the poor in the United States between 1980 and 1989, and their meaning for American democracy. Since the work was first conceived in the mid-1980s, I have relied heavily on the support and encouragement of many people and institutions. In Durham, North Carolina, Allan Kornberg oversaw the development of the first draft of this project, serving as mentor, sounding board, and exemplar of vigorous research. Stephen R. Smith and David Canon contributed much to my understanding of interest groups, social-welfare policy, and the process of political representation in this country. Ray and Dorothy Weathers deserve special thanks. Meanwhile, Duke University provided fellowships and institutional support that allowed me to begin the project.

The work was advanced immeasurably through the infusion of intelligence and insight offered by a National Endowment for the Humanities summer seminar on Political Histories of Collective Action at Cornell University. My understanding of social movements owes much to the example, encouragement, and continuing guidance offered by Sidney Tarrow, and to the insights and challenges offered by David S. Meyer, Karen Beckwith, and the participants in the seminar.

In Las Vegas, James Malek, Michael Bowers, Lawrence Klein, Lori Temple, and Rick Tilman have provided ongoing encouragement, thoughtful advice, and the genesis of a collegial work environment and community in the desert. The Colleges of Liberal Arts and Business at the University of Nevada provided me with research support and with generous leave time to complete the work. I am particularly thankful for awards made through the Center for Advanced Research and by the University Grants and Fellowship Committee. The Nevada Humanities Committee also made a generous grant to aid the completion of the project.

The final draft of the manuscript was completed in the generative and collaborative environment offered by the Program on Nonviolent Sanctions in the Center for International Affairs of Harvard University. CFIA, and PNS in particular, represents a unique environment for scholars to develop and share their research. Doug Bond deserves special thanks for his constant efforts to nurture and support developing research and for his friendship. He also taught me much of what I know about events data development and analysis.

Many other people commented on earlier drafts of this work, as well as on presentations of the various arguments in preparation. These people have contributed much to my understanding of the puzzles explored. In particular, I thank John Schwarz, Anne Costain, Doug McAdam, Andy McFarland, Clark Gibson, and Jeff Berry for the effort they have invested in making me think more carefully and write more clearly. They deserve much credit for making this a better book, as do the anonymous reviewers for the University of Nebraska Press.

Finally, a number of other people deserve special thanks for their years of unflinching support, encouragement, and friendship. Most particularly, I thank Carol Rowley Imig, David Imig, James Nickell, Kathryn Ryder, and Joselyn Zivin. I can only wonder at their continuing patience.

Through the contributions of these people and too many others to name, this work has been completed. Responsibility for its arguments and omissions remains entirely my own.

Introduction

The efforts of antipoverty activists and advocacy groups to combat the Reagan domestic agenda have been widely overlooked, yet they provide examples of active, ideologically based opposition to the Reagan revolution and shed light on one of the principal ways poor Americans gain representation in national politics.

Discussions of democracy usually return to the question of what levels of popular participation are appropriate, necessary, and possible in a society trying to achieve two goals: protecting a set of institutions and processes and ensuring that the state is responsive to the governed. High-school civics texts stress the importance of widespread popular participation in American democracy. Students are taught to recognize the close links between popular participation and popular sovereignty. In college courses, alternative visions of participation are introduced, including in particular procedural or "elitist" theories of democracy, which argue that too much participation—particularly when it is underinformed—is counterproductive to functioning democracies. Students learn of a brand of participatory democracy termed *pluralism,* which offers a market mechanism for political action and decision making. Students are also introduced to the critiques of pluralism, which suggest that it apologizes for a status quo that is glaringly skewed in the direction of the affluent, mainstream, and majoritarian while ignoring the poor, ethnic minorities, and the marginalized. Pluralism, they discover, may overlook many structural reasons for constraints placed on the amount of political involvement of various groups—usually to the advantage of the already advantaged. To paraphrase E. E. Schattschneider, politics is the mobilization of bias. Only certain interests are likely to lead to public mobilization and consideration by decision makers.[1]

Yet even the most vehement critics of American-style pluralism ultimately offer a decidedly pluralistic heaven as their goal. Several responses to contemporary political malaise have been offered, such as intensive civic education to heighten political involvement and changes in rules to equalize political access. The goals of these reforms are the same: to increase levels of informed and committed engagement in the political realm.

To this discussion, I offer another vantage from which to assess the dimensions of political involvement in the United States. This investigation concerns political activity as directed by advocates and activists for the poor and homeless. Poor people in this country provide a test case for questions of popular involvement in politics. Historically, the poor have seldom been active participants in politics. Since 1980 their group interests have been affected in ways that might have incited them to action. Lesser threats incited greater responses from a number of other constituencies during the same period, a phenomenon to which we return. During the 1980s the poor were battered by contractions in both national and local economies combined with marked constriction of federal and state programs and services designed to provide emergency relief as well as long-term support and systemic redress.

President Reagan worked quickly to reverse the dominant trend in social-welfare spending of the previous fifty years not only by retrenching the federal commitment to social welfare but also by working to delegitimate the notion of welfare as an effective response to poverty. The rapid adoption of the Reagan reforms in social-welfare spending, now nearly fifteen years old, presents a case providing telling insights into the conditions under which weak challenging groups are likely to attempt to become directly involved in politics. Perhaps more important, it also demonstrates how political opportunity in the United States is structured so as to anticipate, channel, and potentially dissipate efforts by new groups to enter the polity in any meaningful way.

The story of the response to federal welfare retrenchment offers a mixed set of comments on the possibilities for poor peoples' involvement in politics. It also offers a tentative set of proscriptions for fostering and amplifying such involvement. These findings suggest that political access for the poor is possible but unlikely. The evidence also suggests that dramatic changes in the operating context of American politics will spark both institutional and noninstitutional action by weak groups. This action will seldom gain concessions that extend far beyond the symbolic. Historically, one of the best possibilities for hearing from weak voices in American politics has been through governmental support for advocacy. But this type of patronage is fundamentally flawed. First, it has historically failed to encourage direct participation by poor communities, leaving these groups politically anemic—and dependent on proxy organizations. Second, government sources of grants have seldom been any more supportive than their private counterparts of political-empowerment schemes or "radical" notions of social welfare such as a guaranteed minimum income or right to work. Third, government support has proved to be susceptible to both ideological bias and budget contractions.

This work follows from the premise that increased levels of informed, ongoing participation are the *sine qua non* of viable democracy and that current patterns of participation in the United States are dangerously skewed toward certain groups to the exclusion of many facets of society. Disproportionate patterns of participation entrench disequilibrium in political representation and efficacy.[2] Eroding levels of popular efficacy will ultimately undermine the support for any state, including our own. To counter this trend calls both for the construction of effective social institutions and for actively encouraging widespread, informed participation. The importance of civic education and the role—indeed necessity—of widespread and continuing participation is a theme as old as the Greeks.

However, this work is not a call for a particular brand or level of welfare provision. The types of welfare programs societies construct tell more about the definition of communities than about the needs and characteristics of the poor. These programs are also the outcome of political maneuvering that takes into account many factors beyond helping the poor. I am all too aware of the frailties and convolutions of existing programs to defend them with total conviction. Still, the political discussion of welfare policies is central to the definition of a viable democracy. It is, in effect, the bellwether of how societies decide who will and will not enjoy true and full citizenship. It is possible, however, to be an unabashed advocate of the politics of empowerment and the necessity of universal, active participation without being an apologist for any particular welfare scheme. While this distinction may seem obvious, it is often overlooked and sometimes even reversed: calls for political participation by the poor are often misinterpreted as demands for more welfare programs.

In this work, the voice of the poor is found in advocacy groups and direct-action organizations. Some of these groups predate the New Deal. Most were started either in the 1960s, in response to the War on Poverty, or during the 1980s, in response to the Reagan reforms. In addition to the political actions of advocacy groups, there were several types of direct action undertaken by poor people themselves in alliance with activist groups. The most politically active faction of activists for the poor in the 1980s rallied under the banner of the homeless and launched ongoing civil-disobe-dience campaigns and protest actions over the decade.

Between these two examples of activity, is it fair to say that there has been a movement by the poor and homeless in recent American history? This point is much in dispute. Some students of American social move-ments and public-interest groups have suggested that the events this work chronicles lack the critical dimension of movements.[3] Instead, they argue, advocacy organizations are linked only tenuously to the communities they claim to represent. Over the years, these organizations have drifted away from their movement base and have evolved into more or less mainstream public-interest groups, plying their trade in the nation's capital—living off the government grants gravy train. While these organizations might repre-sent the last vestiges of the civil-rights movement of the 1960s and national welfare-rights movement of the 1970s, their existence fails to provide com-pelling evidence for a political mobilization of the poor today.

Political activists take a different position, arguing that America is even now in the midst of a movement by the poor and homeless, evident in the explosion in the number of homeless shelters across the country and an in-crease in public concern with homelessness. They also point to the grow-ing consensus within the shelter industry that the voice of the poor must be included in shelter operations and planning, and, most important, that shelters are but a small part of a more encompassing political response to homelessness.

Somewhere between these two positions lies the truth about a move-ment for social justice as well as the likelihood of encouraging and main-taining that mobilization and participation. Social observers and social ac-tivists are eager to discuss a number of facets of this phenomenon. What is its relation to the institutions and actors in mainstream political venues? What are the conditions under which this movement has (or might) emerge from and recede into rigid institutionalization? Can a movement exist largely "by proxy," composed of middle-class supporters concerned with some broad notion of social justice and eager to rally alongside low-income people for this collective good? Under what conditions is mobiliza-tion by poor people and their supporters likely? Are there conditions un-der which it is inevitable? Finally, is it possible to look beyond the notion of movements to the ways in which weak and marginalized voices enter into ongoing policy-making processes, across varying levels of interest, mobil-ization, and concern?

Each of these questions, in particular the last, is discussed at some length in this work. By identifying constraints and opportunities confronting advocates for the poor and the strategies and tactics they adopt in response, we learn how weak and peripheralized voices are asserted in the policy process. Further, we can identify ways for weak challenging groups to amplify their own voice, maximize their influence in politics, and increase the likelihood they will continue to be politically active. Toward this end, we seek the structures that channel political action by poor people, the opportunities available for them to become involved in politics, and the strategies they employ to press demands and maximize their policy impact.

THE DIMENSIONS OF THE ARGUMENT

The chapters that follow present the changing situation of both political organizations and direct action by social-justice activists during the 1980s with reference to three questions: What changed in the operating environment of these groups and individuals? How did these changes affect advocacy organizations and protest politics? How did the combination of the efforts of these activists, in turn, create political openings and shape the policy process?

Chapter 1 discusses the formation and political activity of public-interest groups and social-movement organizations and the resources and opportunities available to these groups during the 1980s.

Chapter 2 provides a brief overview of the Reagan administration's agenda for domestic politics and its reception in Congress. The degree to which the White House was able to dismantle the welfare state is explored, as well as the meaning of these federal retrenchments for both certain groups of poor Americans and for organizations working on behalf of poor people's interests.

Chapter 3 traces the historical development of the national hunger lobby, relating its development to episodic waves of welfare reform in this country. Additionally, this chapter discusses the dimensions and resilience of political organizations designed to represent the poor. Why would private-interest groups represent the interests of broad, collective, and forgotten publics such as the poor? Are private-interest groups reliable representatives of the public interest? Chapter 3 also situates poverty fighters in the topography of interest-group representation in the United States, indicating issues most likely to generate group formation and the kinds of groups that emerge in response.

Chapter 4 characterizes the political actions and organizational maneuvering of a sample of pivotal antipoverty advocacy groups. These cases of organizational advocacy are integrated into the then-current political context. The evidence suggests the political activity of these groups follows directly from their level of organizational security. Denied governmental access and previously constant streams of resources, poverty advocates found their organizational resources and tactical arsenals dwindling. This turbulence within their operating environment divided groups in terms of their ability to provide political action.

Chapter 5 examines protest events undertaken by poverty activist groups. Alongside institutional advocates, this second set of political organizations worked to sidestep institutional constraints in order to appeal directly to the public and to the media. These groups played increasingly large roles in the 1980s. Chapter 5 discusses sixty protest events undertaken on behalf of the poor over the 1980s, looking at the tactical repertoire of poor peoples' protest, targets of these actions, and both the intended and unanticipated responses they generated.

Chapter 6 analyzes the mobilization of these interest representatives in terms of the political context in which they arise and the political opportunity structures constraining advocacy for the poor. Why does rising poverty sometimes become a public-policy issue and sometimes not? What relation is apparent between political action in the name of poverty and the increasing salience of poverty as a public-policy issue over the 1980s? Increasing media, expert, and public concern over poverty presumably translated into policy concessions directly through congressional action and indirectly through evermore conciliatory rhetoric. The links among movement action, media attention, issue salience, and both symbolic and tangible government response are explored.

Finally, chapter 7 argues that political context strongly affects the shape and level of interest mobilization. The hunger lobby, made peripheral to many types of institutional politics, was able to amplify its own voice and political action through the positioning of its protests and choice of actions. Both small and large aspects of political opportunity (including legislative routines) limit capacities of insurgents to affect issue attention and policy-making. The contraction of a sector of public-interest representation seldom extinguishes interest in the underlying policy concern, which takes hold in new forms through emergent movements. The surge of mobilization of AIDS advocacy groups and rising interest in the politics of environmental justice, for example, may offer the means for reviving certain facets of a poor people's movement, given the confounding influences of poverty on each of these concerns.

Poverty and Power

Reagan and the Poor: Creating a Policy Crisis and Political Opportunity

During the 1980s in America, the gap between the rich and the poor grew. Today the poor "live in neighborhoods of more concentrated poverty, and include a higher proportion of single mothers and their children" than ever before. A growing percentage of the poor are children isolated from vigorous families and strong neighborhoods. More than 20 percent of all American children live in poverty, and nearly half of all African American children grow up below the poverty line.[1]

Thirty-seven million Americans have no health coverage. Millions are homeless, and tens of millions more lack any income reserves to tide them through a layoff or catastrophic illness. In the 1980s alone, an emerging American underclass was further distanced from the American dream.[2]

Economic conditions during the 1980s exacerbated the already-tenuous position of the poor. A nationwide recession between 1980 and 1982 brought widespread layoffs. In addition, rampant inflation through the 1970s had already eroded the minimum wage to the point where low-paying jobs would not support even a small family, and the job market had become increasingly bifurcated—high-skill, high-tech jobs on the one hand and low-paying, low-skill jobs on the other. This bifurcation precluded advancement for most low-wage workers.

Being poor in the United States means much more than not having a job with high status and high pay. As Nathan Weber notes, between 1985 and 1992, the number of Americans who could not buy enough food to meet their basic nutritional needs rose by almost 50 percent, despite a decline in the number of poor people. In other words, nearly one eighth of all Americans are hungry. Although almost 26 million Americans receive food stamps (more than 10 percent of the population), 6 million people in poverty do not, and 10 million of those who do are still unable to buy enough food. Every month, 20 million Americans must visit food pantries or soup kitchens.[3]

The 1980s were also marked by changes in federal policy toward the poor. The Reagan administration directly challenged federal provision of social support. Federal spending reductions were quickly enacted in 1981 and 1982, with the intention of reshaping the relation between the federal government and the states. In practice, these federal budget cuts reduced both welfare provision and support to the states in an attempt to scale back the size and scope of the federal government and to alter dramatically its mission from ensurer of opportunity to defender of the market.

What effect did these economic and policy changes have on the politics of poverty and on the political activity of poor people and their supporters? Where was the political voice of poor Americans through the 1980s?

Direct political action, in the form of interest groups and protest politics, is one of the most important ways disfranchised Americans come to be heard. The ways in which low-income Americans became active in politics during the 1980s highlight the opportunities for participation in America. Conversely, instances in which representative groups for the poor failed to coalesce and take action mark the boundaries of their participation.

THE AMERICAN POOR

It is difficult to talk about "the poor" in the United States because of the many cleavages in the category. In 1992, 14.5 percent (36.9 million people) of the total U.S. population lived in poverty. The poverty rate was highest among female-headed families with children, with some 48.3 percent of these families living in poverty in 1992. Among American children, nearly 22 percent (14.6 million) were impoverished. In addition to children and single mothers, ethnic minorities disproportionately suffer from poverty. In particular, the black poverty rate has remained above 30 percent since 1959, and the poverty rate for Hispanics has hovered around 30 percent during the 1980s and early 1990s. At the same time, a majority of the poverty population (66.5 percent) is white.[4] For all these reasons, it is most accurate to say that many different groups of Americans are poor.

We also find many different paths to poverty. Americans become impoverished through unemployment, illness or disease, economic dislocations, and abandonment. Their condition is worsened by homelessness, deinstitutionalization, and single motherhood. The diversity of low-income Americans helps to explain the historical paucity of political action by the poor. To act as a group, poor people would need to see themselves as undergoing a common plight—yet they have little or no opportunity to recognize the shared aspects of their condition.

ADVOCACY AND ACTIVISM FOR THE POOR

This book investigates the development and operation of two types of political advocacy for poor Americans. The first type of advocacy is found in the network of organizations that constitute the "hunger lobby" active in national politics. Information on the stability and political activity of groups in the hunger lobby has been collected through interviews, annual reports, and financial information, including tax returns. Together, these different sources describe the organizational situation and political activity of public-interest advocacy groups. Additionally, twenty-one current and former representatives of groups within the hunger lobby generously consented to interviews. In return, they were guaranteed a degree of anonymity (as is standard in social-science practice). In each case, the conclusions drawn from the public record are corroborated with the observations of these group representatives.

A second type of advocacy is found in the less institutionalized organizations that came to play an increasingly important role in poverty advocacy over the decade through "outsider" tactics and direct political action. This aspect of the investigation is informed by interviews as well as data generated from nationwide media accounts of events, drawing from an encompassing set of national newspapers and opinion magazines available online through the Lexis/Nexis data-information service. On-line archival databases offer much promise for collecting events data. The Nexis service, for example, compiles more than fifty thousand full-text news articles each year.

To gauge levels of mobilization on public-policy issues, we can look to both the health of advocacy organizations and the levels and type of action undertaken by activists. Two fundamental characteristics of social movements are a set of political organizations and a series of spontaneous activities beyond the control of these organizations.

Applying a social-movement framework to the analysis of poverty advocacy offers a set of tools for looking at this type of direct political action, often shunted to the margins of studies of political behavior, and provides a standard of "movement" against which to measure levels of mobilization by and for the poor. Matching public-interest groups with social movements also recognizes the distinction between economically oriented groups and their public-interest counterparts. While economically oriented groups mobilize members through selective incentives and constraints, public-interest groups (like social movements) have few such incentives or constraints to deploy.[5]

Political and social movements use various means, including both insti-

tutional channels and extrainstitutional political action, to pursue their political goals. In this respect, movements exist in a dynamic state of interaction with the political mainstream.[6] Movements arise when activists and
organizations "mobilize and apply their resources, including supporters,
money, the force of the law, legitimacy and communications networks, to
their political purposes."[7]

RESOURCES NECESSARY FOR MOVEMENTS

The resources held by potential challengers are critical to the process of social-
movement emergence. Necessary resources include a capacity for organizing—
allowing activists to communicate with each other, with potential supporters,
and with the media and political institutions. Additionally, movement mobilization is much more likely under particular operating conditions, or "structures of
opportunity." Where such structures are favorable, movements seem inevitable.
At other times, their emergence appears impossible.

Although widespread discontent attracts individuals to movements, it
does not explain the ability of movements to mobilize. Instead, the generation of insurgency more closely follows from increases in the level of resources available and changes in political context rather than from the general level of discontent within the aggrieved group.[8]

The dimensions of collective action for social justice are broader than often sketched. Activist groups such as the Community for Creative Non-
Violence orchestrate demonstrations in which thousands of citizens, including hundreds of homeless people, hold a sit-in in the Capitol rotunda.
At the same time, groups with related agendas but different institutional
linkages and greater access to decision making can arrange to bring Aid to
Families with Dependent Children (AFDC) beneficiaries before congressional hearings to testify against the "welfare queen" caricature who provided a target for Reagan-era budget cutters.

Examining both political inputs indicates the potential for movements to
mobilize a broad range of groups with independent resources and
strengths. Social-movement organizations and public-interest groups rely
on tangible resources such as money, space to congregate and conduct
business, and a means of publicizing the movement's existence and ideas.
Other critical resources include paid staff and volunteers.[9]

Resources flow toward movements from the constituency that stands
to benefit from the mobilization, from a conscience constituency, or from
institutions.[10] Movements for the poor rely on conscience constituents
and on institutional resources, particularly from government and foundation grants. Public and institutional support remains uncertain, how-

ever, since it fluctuates with public opinion and foundation priorities. Private corporations and foundations (as well as state and federal agencies) extend grants to advocates and activists when doing so appears urgent. The 1992 Los Angeles riots, for example, led to renewed, though ambiguous, calls for private and governmental investment in poor people's care and programs.

Another resource at the disposal of social-justice advocates in the 1980s was an identifiable antagonist. As Jo Freeman notes, "A solid opponent can do more to unify a group . . . than any other factor."[11] Such a figure provides a lightning rod for mobilization. The Reagan administration's welfare-bashing rhetoric and policy agenda gave advocates a ready target.

COMMUNITIES AND SOCIAL-MOVEMENT DEVELOPMENT

Movements arise within communities and depend on communal linkages. In one sense, this means that movements adopt the "organizational patterns of a community."[12] More broadly, it implies that movements are constrained by the "values, past experiences, reference groups, and expectations" of their members.[13] It also means that movements can draw the fierce resolve of people defending their homes and families and, conversely, that they wither where community identity fails to develop.

For collective action to appear logical to potential participants and interested bystanders, it must fit established communal norms. Challengers draw support and legitimacy when they are seen as protecting shared ideals and trusted institutions. For these reasons, it is important for insurgents to make clear how their cause is tied to broader social forces.[14] Challengers can invoke a connection with accepted and established social movements, dominant religious beliefs, civic ideals, and the law. Civil-rights protesters, for example, were able to connect their appeals to the foundations of American identity, to the dictates of the law, and to widely shared religious ideals.

People are more likely to become involved in a movement when it coincides with their values, sense of community, and past experiences. That communities are critical to collective action also highlights the importance of groups for movements. Groups bring individuals together and nurture the seeds of democratic change by creating environments in which people are able to craft "a deeper and more assertive group identity."[15] Challengers working to mobilize support can enlist communal associations (e.g., sympathetic church congregations), or they can create their own organizations (e.g., building pit camps where striking miners can congregate, exchange information, and plan and carry out collective protest).[16]

ORGANIZATIONS IN SOCIAL MOVEMENTS

Successful political movements invoke preexisting organizations and generate new groups in the process of mobilization. Organizations offer a venue in which to develop collective consciousness, formulate strategy, and take action.[17] In fact, collective interests ordinarily cannot be maintained "unless there is a welding of spontaneous groups into stable organizations."[18] At the most tangible level, organizations offer challengers four critical resources: members, established structures of solidary incentives, communications networks, and leaders.[19] Put another way, organizations can forge a community for collective action—bringing people together, making them realize their common complaint, identifying their mutual antagonist, offering encouragement for their collective efforts, and affirming the justness of their cause. In this way, organizations link otherwise atomized individuals, making collective action possible.

The most viable and effective social-movement mobilizations draw from a range of organizations with different resources and compatible objectives.[20] Exploiting a range of organizations allows various access routes to government and resources from public, corporate, and foundation patrons, consequently providing more strategic options.

Critics note that organizations inevitably draw support and energy away from the reforming potential of protest. Organizations may consequently prove to be too conservative to advance movement goals and thus more useful to elite supporters than to the movements they claim to represent.[21] Certainly, organizations work both to guarantee their incomes and to secure linkages with foundation and corporate funders.[22] Consequently, institutionalized groups are unwilling to stray too far from the concerns and beliefs of their funders. Under unusual circumstances, this conservatism may actually solidify the alliance between the public-interest advocacy community and movement challengers, which may find themselves threatened by shifts in the direction of public policy. Additionally, even the most institutionalized groups can provide the infrastructure for later cycles of mobilization.

In these respects, social movements include both protest politics and interest-group activity. While public-interest groups work through institutional channels and avoid more dramatic public protests, their energy contributes to the formation and adoption of movement goals. Moreover, when insurgents are inactive or go unnoticed, organized interest groups may continue to help shape incremental politics.

ORGANIZATIONS AND INSTITUTIONAL LINKAGES

Organizations bring different histories and elite linkages to social movements. These aspects of organizational identity, in turn, define and mediate the relation between organization supporters and movement forces.

Useful organizations may include groups that have survived from earlier iterations of the movement—which may share many of the same goals as new movement activists. This link, however, is not ensured. The second generation of the women's movement illustrates the potential difficulty in forging connections with older groups, which may differ on strategy and identity.[23] Similarly, organizations founded during the southern wave of the civil-rights movement were uneasy about embracing later vestiges of the movement couched in terms of black power.[24]

A second set of organizations that may be pressed into service are church groups. Churches have long functioned as halfway houses for social reform in the United States.[25] Doug McAdam notes the importance of the infrastructure provided by church congregations for the mobilization of the civil-rights movement.[26] Similarly, American Protestant reformers led the call for government intervention in welfare, public education, and child labor. More recently, in the sanctuary movement American congregations have provided asylum for Latin American refugees. The broad range of churches in this country maintain an equally broad set of relations with political activists. Movements draw from different religious groups and, consequently, different types and levels of resources, and concurrently face varied strategic and policy constraints imposed by these organizational linkages.

In addition to preexisting organizations, movements spawn new ones. As Sidney Tarrow notes, during a period of increased mobilization, existing organized groups will begin to mobilize while the unorganized will begin to organize—leading to the resurgence of dormant groups and the emergence of new groups.[27] A period of mobilization thus means that funds and members flow toward existing organizations and new groups form.[28]

More broadly, organizations become central to the process of interest mobilization first because of their resources. Second, they are critical to defining relations between elite supporters and challengers. Third, groups are crucial to identifying the "community interests" that are the most powerful base of mobilization.[29] Finally, movements are operationally defined in terms of their resources, strategic action, and constraints. Each of these aspects are mediated through critical movement organizations.

POLITICAL OPPORTUNITY STRUCTURES AND COLLECTIVE ACTION

Along with the level and type of resources held by challengers, the political context and institutional structures in a society shape the opportunities for dissent and channel its expression. Political opportunity structures are dimensions of the political environment structuring the incentives for people to undertake collective action. These resources *external* to challenging groups include openings in levels of political access, "shifts in ruling alignments, the availability of influential allies, and cleavages within and among elites."[30] Various levels of government have a say in whether protest will be allowed and in the types of response it will generate. As Peter Eisinger demonstrates, a complete lack of tolerance for dissent will drive protest underground, decreasing the likelihood of peaceful challenge and increasingly pushing insurgents toward terrorism. At the other extreme, completely open and accessible governments preempt protest altogether.[31] In their response to dissent, governments can repress mobilization as well as facilitate less threatening forms of participation. McAdam has shown, for example, that a decline in the number of lynchings in the 1930s provided black Americans with space to begin building stronger indigenous political organizations. By the 1960s, expanding venues for black political participation in both urban politics and the Democratic party split the civil-rights movement, with one faction seeking incremental gains and another committed to extrainstitutional protest.[32] Similar examples of insurgent movements relying on political factors have been noted for the women's movement, the farm workers' movement, the antinuclear movement, and the poor people's movement.[33]

In fact, movements by and for the poor may be particularly susceptible to the constraining influence of political context because of the lack of indigenous resources, organizations, and infrastructure undergirding their efforts. But political opportunity is more than a simple function of relatively static institutions. Levels of opportunity also depend on the degree of support insurgents receive from policy and policymakers as well as other participants in the policy process.[34] The degree to which the public perceives an issue to be societal in nature and appropriate to political response, for example, will shape the degree to which it becomes *politically salient*, deserving space on political agendas. In turn, the ways in which issues are perceived depend on how they are framed and presented to the public and the levels of *elite support* they generate. Important elite supporters can bring different resources to movements, such as expertise or institutional legitimacy. Media personalities can provide movements with celebrity, vitality, and mainstream recognition. More broadly, elite supporters help give voice and attention to dissident movements.[35]

The actions of other social groups can also dramatically affect the likelihood of protest and its expansion to widespread concern. President Reagan's belligerence toward the Soviet Union, for example, provided a rallying point for supporters of the nuclear freeze, as Americans' fear of nuclear war rose.[36]

Critical to the process of expanding political opportunity is the size of the rift between expectations and social arrangements. When the existing political order fails to provide expected patterns of access to challengers, the legitimacy of governing coalitions and institutions is questioned. Eroding legitimacy contributes to an environment in which people are more likely to feel outraged, entitled, and more likely to participate in movement activity.[37]

There are a number of conditions under which legitimacy begins to break down. When policy-making veers in a new and ambiguously supported direction, for example, support not only for a particular policy but also for the initiating governing party, coalition, or institution may begin to erode. Similarly, when widely accepted measures for righting economic or social imbalance fail, political legitimacy is undermined. When accepted self-correcting mechanisms in the economy failed to reverse the Great Depression, for example, political space was opened for a new vision of the relation between government intervention and economic recovery, leading to the New Deal realignment and the ascendence of Keynesian economics in national policy-making. In the 1980s, the link between general economic growth and overall recovery seemed to break, as widespread economic recovery failed to diminish the magnitude and prevalence of poverty.

In both cases, fissures in the existing social contract held the potential for undermining "the system." These fissures include cases in which government agents undermine or remove existing and expected programs and in which expected processes fail to materialize (e.g., general economic recovery does not raise general welfare).

In the same way, when new political alignments and policy directions leave constituents and groups without a clear sense of where traditionally handled claims should be channeled, governmental legitimacy can erode as expected responses are not forthcoming. The rift between expected and actual patterns of political response can undermine legitimacy, leading to calls for accommodation and change.

SPEAKING OUT: PLURALIST THEORY AND THE POOR

American democratic theory holds that groups sharing common grievances will unite to press demands for reform. James Madison argued that Americans would inevitably band into factions to rally against their common adversaries.[38] Open and easy access to political institutions encourages fluid alignments of interest advocates in the United States. American political institutions are constructed to be insulated from political pressures while allowing enough access to preempt powerful and destabilizing extrainstitutional dissent. The resulting political structure divides power into distinct yet interdependent pieces, fashioning a system with many access points for political involvement.[39]

This institutional structure allows disturbances to the status quo, such as emerging political issues and constituents, to spark the "spontaneous" coalescence of individual interests, leading to the formation of more or less formal groups of issue representatives. These groups, in turn, compete for access and influence in American politics. Consequently, citizens with politically relevant concerns band together, directing their collective energy and resources to coax a favorable response from government. Interests that strike a chord with the public have the capacity to generate group formation, and no group lacks the basic resources necessary to coalesce and seek government access. By this logic, group formation becomes the basic test of legitimacy for policy preferences in American society.[40]

This traditional vision of American democracy and group participation overstates the possibility for group organization and political involvement. The resources needed to organize and maintain political interest groups are not equally available to all potential challengers. In consequence, many issue positions do not develop organized representatives, leaving a universe of representative groups skewed toward particular visions of the public interest. One factor accounting for the direction of this skew is the presence of wealthy benefactors—at times including the federal government—who have an interest in underwriting the cost of group formation for particular organizations. The system of representation that results from this process of group formation is, consequently, characterized by lapses and redundancies of representation.[41]

POVERTY AND POLITICAL QUIESCENCE

The poor seldom "spontaneously coalesce" to generate collective action. In fact, the likelihood of political involvement in the United States seems to relate directly to socioeconomic status, with the more affluent more likely to participate.[42] The poor by definition lack the financial resources to devote to political action. In addition, poor Americans as a group are generally hampered by low levels of education, are distanced from all but the most basic communications systems, lack indigenous organizations, and have little opportunity to identify collectively. For a group to pursue its common interest, as we have seen above, members must recognize their common identity, believe they share a collective complaint, and target an external antagonist.[43]

The absence of class consciousness in the United States follows, in part, from the ways Americans view politics and themselves. Americans seldom differentiate among themselves by class—preferring to link themselves to a large and amorphous group known as the middle class.[44] Second, regardless of their income, Americans seldom view government as responsible for individual and community-level economic problems. Instead, blame for individual troubles tends to be placed either on a lack of individual initiative or on some type of general economic malaise.[45] At another level, Americans seldom link economic malaise with government action, instead believing strongly in the ethic of self-reliance.[46] The notion of self-reliance also delegitimates collective action by the poor by viewing the poor as responsible for their own poverty and hinders efforts to organize middle-class support for issues of social justice.

This ethic of self-reliance means that poor Americans tend to participate less in the political process, believing they should invest their time in looking for work rather than in political action. In the 1940s, Wight Bakke found that few poor Americans belonged to political organizations and that, in fact, "political action does not rank high among the tactics adopted by the unemployed as a means for solving their problems."[47] Writing nearly forty years later about the political involvement of the unemployed, Kay Schlozman and Sidney Verba note the same political alienation among low-income Americans.[48] Similarly, Jennifer Hochschild finds that poor Americans have as little faith in government interventions in poverty as do more affluent respondents.[49]

Poor people, then, are unlikely to band together, and few organized representative groups focus on securing political change to benefit the poor.[50] For all these reasons, it is all the more surprising to find the range of political organizations that have emerged to provide advocacy for the poor. Rather than arise from within poor communities, many of these groups organized in response to heightened public interest in social justice during the New Deal and Great Society eras, taking advantage of resources made available by private foundations and the federal government. Heavily reliant on federal and foundation grants, these groups have provided national-level advocacy, organizational support, and an infrastructure for mobilization.[51] These organizations and their actions are fundamental to understanding contemporary mobilizations by the poor as well as the constraints on activism on behalf of the poor. (I return to a more complete investigation of the resources, organizational constraints, and political activity of organized representatives of social justice in chapters 3 and 4.)

Over the years, a large and diverse collection of groups and individuals have taken up the cause of poverty, including organized labor, ecumenical and civil-rights organizations, city and state governments, federal agencies, and politically active groups at great risk of poverty, such as the elderly. It is logical that these same groups would provide the first line of defense against the Reagan agenda.

Many of these traditional partners in the hunger lobby, however, were absent over the 1980s, an absence which needs explanation. Some allies of the poor were diverted from the coalition by concerns closer to home, either in the form of policy attacks or organizational threats. Still other allies were bought off, dissipating their protest.

Notably absent from the hunger lobby were civil-rights organizations. In the United States, race has played a critical role in fostering collective identification. During the 1960s, African Americans translated their collective experience into calls for political equality and economic opportunity through the civil-rights movement.[52] While race has heightened calls for solidarity in the name of social justice, collective action has seldom crossed racial lines.

In the 1970s, the civil-rights movement was divided by internal fissures and by a conservative backlash against affirmative action. The Supreme Court decision in *Regents of the University of California* v. *Bakke* and battles over busing further confused the role of race in American politics. Jacqueline Pope notes class and gender (along with racial) divisions in the welfare-rights movements during the late 1960s and early 1970s.[53] "The welfare rights arena was virtually devoid of any African-American and Caribbean clergy or middle-class participation."[54] Representatives of welfare-rights organizations attributed this absence to a combination of class bias (middle-class blacks were ashamed of the welfare-rights activities) and gender bias (the movement was largely made up of women).[55]

The fragmenting potential of race was particularly evident during the Reagan-Bush era. Republican rhetoric painted the Democrats, and consequently the coalition of groups they claimed to represent, as the party of extremism—hijacked by fringe elements advocating high taxes and preferential treatment for minorities.[56] This rhetorical attack on the coalitions constituting the Left struck a chord with middle-class and working-class white voters (the Reagan Democrats). Meanwhile, civil-rights organizations themselves faced political attacks from Justice Department appointees eager to halt the enforcement of civil-rights legislation.

Another traditional ally of the poor has been organized labor. Labor unions have long provided the most powerful and influential advocacy for large-scale, universalistic social-welfare programs in the United States. Advances in social welfare, consequently, have historically occurred when the labor movement has been strongest.[57]

Labor and the poor, however, make uneasy allies, since many of the poor are unemployed and therefore not union members. Nevertheless, labor has traditionally been at the forefront of lobbying efforts for the poor. The 1970s Humphrey-Hawkins Comprehensive Education and Training Act was championed by a coalition of unions, civil-rights groups, and religious organizations. Thirty years earlier, this same coalition had fought for passage of the Full Employment Act. In consequence, the ramifications of labor setbacks in the 1980s reverberated well beyond labor, undermining union support for many causes that had relied on union patronage. Assaults on labor meant fewer grants and organizational support from labor to poor people's groups and forced labor's own lobbying efforts inward, that is, toward their own concerns rather than toward the poor.[58] This was evident throughout the 1980s, when, for example, the amount of grant money from the American Federation of Labor–Council of Industrial Organizations (AFL-CIO) to antipoverty organizations was cut.[59]

Without these allies, the poor were left with political access largely through direct action or through proxy advocacy groups.

SOCIAL MOVEMENTS AND INTEREST GROUPS FOR THE POOR

This chapter has introduced the major tangible and intangible resources available to social-movement organizations and public-interest groups and has discussed the ways in which movements and groups develop and evolve in response to the opportunities and constraints they face. The range of organizational forms and strategic actions that have developed in turn define the opportunities for direct representation of the poor in American politics and thereby explain the ways marginalized voices are heard in American society.

Chapter 2 reviews the policy initiatives of the early 1980s and their effect on low-income people in this country. The chapter argues that the Reagan reforms threatened the welfare of the poor in ways that might have been expected to spark a mobilization in support of social justice.

2

The Reagan Revolution in
Domestic Spending

During the 1980s, the political opportunity structures confronting representatives for the poor fluctuated markedly. The Reagan administration combined budget cuts with a belligerent rhetorical position toward welfare recipients—both providing a target for activists for the poor and undermining the presumption engrained in postwar welfare programs that welfare was generally a worthy cause. In addition to these dramatic policy and rhetorical shifts, a deep recession between 1980 and 1982 increased the number of people in poverty to its highest levels since the early 1960s. The recovery from this recession, even though in many respects robust and long-lasting, failed to boost the poorest members of society, thus exacerbating the divide in economic well-being and social opportunity.

In response, public attention to poverty rose, directed toward the combination of cuts to social-service programs, a rhetorical attack on the poor, a strong and clearly identifiable antagonist in the White House, a bruising economic recession, and the unevenness of the recovery, which failed to reach the poor. This failure went far toward confirming the mean spiritedness of the White House, which was blamed for much of the increase in poverty among children and families, and implicated the Reagan administration in undermining the American social contract with the poor.[1]

In this social contract, support for the poor, while miserly, was seemingly guaranteed. Since the Great Society, welfare had become figuratively and, in certain respects, literally an "entitlement." Not only was this relation under siege, but the alternative offered by the White House—widespread economic well-being through decreased governmental parasitism—failed to materialize, as evident in both the immediate recession and lopsided recovery. All these factors expanded the opportunities available to supporters of social-justice programs eager to generate public and political response to halt the Reagan agenda. This combination of factors also meant that the relative bargaining position of the poor and their supporters was in transition through the decade. An improved bargaining position for the aggrieved generally raises the cost of repressing insurgents and increases the likelihood that their issues will gain institutional consideration.[2]

However, on several levels, it is unclear whether this process applies to the poor. After all, they became the target of administration cost-cutting measures precisely because they could easily be treated as scapegoats. But this take on the situation is an oversimplification. First, general levels of concern with poverty, as distinct from welfare, remained high over the decade. Second, media and public concern with poverty grew to include homelessness and child poverty, exacerbated by the burgeoning prevalence of homelessness and the changing face of the poor. In this respect, the administration's claims to have maintained the safety net for the "truly needy" became increasingly suspect in the face of seemingly deserving, or at least increasingly familiar, poor people.[3]

But two shrewd maneuvers counterbalanced the expansion of opportunity suggested by this set of circumstances. First, social-welfare cuts spared the elderly—historically the only group of Americans *both* likely to be poor and politically active. From the 1970s on, poverty among the aged continued to drop, even as the poverty rate for almost all other social groups grew. This political maneuver circumvented the possibility of a concerted opposition from the "gray lobby."[4]

Second, much of the administration's cuts in social-welfare programs hit discretionary rather than entitlement spending. The programs cut, including the Legal Services Corporation (LSC) and the Community Services Administration (CSA), had provided much of the support for advocacy organizations. Consequently, the Omnibus Budget Reconciliation Acts (OBRA) cuts reduced political action for the poor immediately—by defunding advocacy organizations—as well as over the long term through the potential role of these groups in forming an organizational network for mobilization on behalf of social justice.

THE IMPLEMENTATION OF THE REAGAN AGENDA

In 1981, President Ronald Reagan inherited an array of domestic social-welfare problems: high unemployment, disappearance of assembly jobs to foreign manufacturers, loss of service-economy jobs held by native-born Americans to immigrants, and a bulge in the labor supply created by the baby-boom generation.[5] In addition, the minimum wage had fallen consistently in real value, so that many low-paying jobs failed to keep a family above the poverty line.[6] As a result, increasing numbers of employed Americans remained poor.

The Reagan administration worked quickly to enact three broad economic and social-policy transformations. First, the White House sought to scale back the income-redistribution policies of the previous half century while maintaining assistance to the "truly needy." In so doing, the administration worked to change the character and scope of welfare programs by reducing federal involvement in social services. Second, the administration attempted to rejuvenate the economy through a massive overhaul of the tax code, removing taxes it believed were serious disincentives to hard work and investment. Third, the president tried to bolster American security by continuing the military programs adopted during the Carter presidency and adding a variety of new programs, including the Strategic Defense Initiative.[7]

Immediately setting to work on his domestic agenda, President Reagan presented to Congress in 1981 a series of budget cuts concentrated in two areas: entitlement programs for the poor and operating grants to state and local government.[8] This combination followed from the administration's desire to curtail the growth and pervasiveness of government spending even though the bulk of domestic expenditures is concentrated in a handful of entitlement programs that are extremely difficult if not politically impossible to cut, such as Social Security retirement benefits and Medicare. These programs benefit the elderly, whose numbers and political allies in the government (including President Reagan) gave them considerable power. As a result, more vulnerable programs without strong political allies, including Medicaid, food stamps, and AFDC, bore the brunt of the budget cuts.[9]

Reagan promised cuts in spending without affecting programs for the truly needy by tightening eligibility requirements for AFDC and food stamps and by capping state spending for Medicaid. Through these changes, the administration sought to wean potential workers from welfare and in the process to provide them with new and powerful incentives to work. By instituting a system of punishments (e.g., more stringent inclusion requirements), the welfare dependency of able-bodied workers would theoretically diminish.

Dramatic reductions in federal investment in social services coupled with deepening recession had a number of effects on the poverty population. First, fewer services were available to increasing numbers of poor people. Particularly hard hit were those who were recent additions to the poverty rolls and those approaching the poverty line. These groups were excluded from food stamps, AFDC, and the school-lunch program. Second, long-term poverty increased as low-income people were forced deeper into destitution before qualifying for assistance. Third, administrative budgets for departments of social services were cut and penalties for errors were increased, making it extremely difficult for social services to take on new applicants. Fourth, accepting assistance became more stigmatized as the White House led the rhetorical charge against welfare abuse.[10]

The administration's changes in social-welfare programs and tax policies and the subsequent increase in poverty meant that "almost half of the overall poverty increase and almost two-thirds of the child poverty increase between 1979 and 1989 was due to changes in governmental policy. Governmental policy increased poverty significantly during the 1980–82 recession. . . . This is not surprising given that welfare policy was tightened during this same period."[11]

While the Reagan administration was not the first to seek reductions in the size and scope of the federal government, it remains unrivaled in the sweep of the cuts it enacted through the 1981 and 1982 budgets. Federal spending was cut by more than $35 billion in 1981 alone. Nearly 70 percent of the total came from programs for the poor.[12]

"The Great Society, built and consolidated over fifteen years, was shrunk to size in just 26 hours and 12 minutes of floor debate," observed *Newsweek*.[13] Means-tested assistance programs were cut by 54 percent, while nonentitlement programs such as housing subsidies were cut by $32 billion, after adjustment for inflation. Job training was reduced by 81 percent, housing assistance for the elderly and handicapped by 47 percent, and legal services for the poor by 28 percent.

Meanwhile, the Reagan tax plan, enacted by Congress in August 1981, cut rates by 25 percent over three years. While critics charged that this tax policy favored the rich and the budget cuts hurt the poor, congressional Democrats offered little opposition. Southern and conservative Democrats staunchly supported the president's program while liberal members of Congress were subdued by their fears of the president's popularity and by a projected Republican sweep in the upcoming 1982 congressional elections. Members of Congress found themselves either forced to support the Reagan agenda or to defend "the failed policies of the past."[14]

Emboldened by his legislative success, Reagan proceeded to attack other facets of the Great Society. He appointed conservatives to the attorney general's office, the Civil Rights Commission, the Justice Department, and the Equal Employment Opportunity Commission. Subsequently, the Justice Department quit bringing school and housing segregation cases to court.

Meanwhile, prodevelopment appointees to the Department of the Interior, including Anne Gorsuch and James Watt, proposed that up to eighty million acres of federal lands be turned over to private developers by the year 2000.

The recession of 1982 exacerbated the effects of tax and benefit cuts. Industrial production plunged while unemployment rosters swelled. Strict monetary policies undercut the automobile and steel industries while car sales fell to their lowest levels in twenty years. Meanwhile, housing starts hit a fifteen-year low and businesses went bankrupt 42 percent faster than in 1980. States with heavy industry saw the highest unemployment rates, particularly among blue-collar workers, women, and minorities. To pay for military increases despite reduced tax revenue, the administration employed deficit spending. Instead of the promised balanced budget, Reagan's tax cut escalated the federal deficit to $2 trillion. Deficit spending was even more attractive since it left no room in the budget for social services. Budget director David Stockman conceded that the deficit meant lower taxes on the rich while squeezing out the Left.[15]

The Reagan cuts, coupled with tax breaks, produced one of the quickest and most regressive redistributions of wealth in U.S. history. In contrast to its rhetoric about removing government from financial life, "the Reagan government injected itself more enthusiastically into the economy than any administration since Lyndon Johnson's Great Society. Indeed, Reagan's administration took so much money from the pockets of middle- and lower-income Americans and shoved it up to the wealthiest 10 percent in our society that a top-heavy structure now threatens to come crashing down on us."[16]

Few groups among the poor escaped the budget ax. While liberals blew the whistle on the administration for attempting to gut the school-lunch program (e.g., by counting ketchup and pickle relish as vegetables), there was little public outcry over the removal of about 500,000 students from the free-meal program. Without the assurance of a certain number of federally subsidized lunches, many school districts were unable to continue providing meals. In practice, greater numbers of children were left without a daily lunch or breakfast.[17]

Social services for other groups among the poor were also dismantled. The Reagan administration cut the principal agent of federal job training, the Comprehensive Employment and Training Act, by more than $5.5 billion, reducing training and jobs for increasing numbers of unemployed, displaced, and obsolete workers. Similarly, despite increasing media stories of pervasive homelessness, the number of federally subsidized dwellings was pruned and rents were raised on remaining units. Public-housing budgets were reduced by $9.5 billion by 1982.[18] According to Edward Lazere and his colleagues, the 1980s saw severe cuts in federal housing programs.[19] As Christopher Jencks notes, in the same decade budget authorizations fell dramatically overall, though Congress quietly maintained outlay levels over much of the decade.[20]

Tighter eligibility requirements meant decreasing rates of participation in federal programs despite increasing poverty rates. Participation in the AFDC program actually dropped from 11.1 million in 1981 to 10.4 million in 1982 while the country faced the highest poverty rate since 1963. Almost all families with earnings of any kind were denied AFDC and related support, including health benefits. Moreover, social-services agencies lost their outreach budgets and faced stiff penalties for overpayments, undermining their willingness to extend benefits.[21]

Proponents of federal retrenchments cheered on these cuts and joined the rhetorical attack on welfare. A Heritage Foundation report from the early 1980s argued that increased use of soup kitchens and other emergency services was an affirmative response to the president's cuts, demonstrating that a well-established network of privately provided services ensured that truly hungry people were fed.[22] In more sweeping terms, Attorney General Edwin Meese dismissed reports of hunger in America as "anecdotal," while the president publicly charged that the welfare system was plagued by "waste, fraud and abuse."[23]

POLICY UPHEAVAL: STEAMROLLING DOMESTIC CONSENSUS

The Reagan administration claimed that strong electoral majorities favored cuts in government, and Democrats remained hesitant to oppose what appeared to be widely popular cost-cutting measures. Members of Congress, regardless of ideology, were reluctant to square off against the president on poverty-program cuts throughout most of the Reagan era. As a result, over the early part of the decade, most congressional attention to poverty was concentrated on ways to cut welfare spending. The beleaguered welfare state bore the brunt of the Reagan administration's suspicion that "waste, fraud and abuse" plagued government bureaucracy, particularly social services—and in turn that welfare was responsible for domestic economic malaise.

Reluctant to challenge the president's initiatives, Congress strongly endorsed two of the administration's major spending proposals in 1981, approving a $37.7 billion tax cut and pruning $35.2 billion from the reconciliation budget. In addition, they approved block grants designed to redirect responsibility for social services to the states, launching the administration's "swap and turn back" initiatives.[24]

One of the most significant changes enacted in 1981 was the abolition of the CSA and a significant rollback in the LSC. Although much of the funding for the programs formerly administered by the CSA was rolled into other programs for fiscal years 1982–86, the end of the agency signified two changes in federal involvement in social services. Symbolically, the loss of CSA announced the federal government was no longer interested in taking the lead in social justice, redirecting the focus of responsibility for social welfare to the states. At the same time, the end of CSA and cuts to the LSC meant that little federal grant money would be available to advocacy organizations and contract agencies concerned with long-term and systemic poverty relief. These organizations, particularly legal-services support agencies, had been tremendously effective at winning court cases forcing state and federal governments to live up to their statutory obligations to care for the poor.[25]

In 1982, Congress approved continued social-services rollbacks, cutting federal welfare programs by an additional $1.1 billion. Although these reductions fell short of the Reagan administration's targets, they continued the significant and abrupt changes in the direction of domestic welfare spending. Congressional action followed the president's directives for budget reconciliation by cutting the core of federal welfare programs. This second round of cuts hit the AFDC program, child-support enforcement provisions, and the Supplemental Security Income (SSI) program. Congressional changes in 1982 increased "workfare" provisions and tightened AFDC eligibility requirements. Further, strict penalties were enacted for states with enrollment errors above 4 percent. This change meant that already-harried departments of social services became extremely uneasy about extending benefits to new applicants.[26]

After the 1982 elections, which failed to bring the predicted wave of new Republican legislators, congressional enthusiasm for the Reagan domestic agenda began to chill noticeably. Democrats held their majority in the House of Representatives, and public-opinion polls showed rising uneasiness with the direction of Reagan's domestic policy. In 1983, the U.S. Conference of Mayors reported that, "although there are several emergency problems of concern to the mayors at this time, hunger is probably the most prevalent and the most insidious."[27] Congressman Leon Panetta of California reported to the House of Representatives that "the use of soup kitchens, food pantries and hunger centers is up dramatically in the past two years, in some areas by 400 to 500 percent."[28] At the same time, soup kitchens reported turning away two to three people for every one person served.[29]

The year 1983 also brought a stream of news stories about hunger and poverty in America's cities and suburbs. Churches, charities, representatives of American cities, and advocacy groups for the poor produced stacks of reports showing that emergency food-distribution centers were overwhelmed by growing demand for their services. These reports pointed to the increasing number of families seeking emergency aid and growing number of elderly people who found their food budgets were squeezed by Medicare changes, forcing them to devote more money to medical bills.[30] Congress responded to these reports by calling more frequent hearings on hunger in America and gradually extending the scope of the commodity-donation program.

The White House moved quickly to counter critics of its domestic agenda, claiming that these reports were anecdotal and the work of left-wing activists. For example, a widely cited Food Research Action Center report summarizing many of the city and regional reports on increasing hunger in America was characterized by budget director David Stockman as "absolutely, totally and completely untrue." From the bully pulpit of the White House, the administration argued that critics were purposely ignoring rising federal spending on food aid. Further, it argued that many new clients of food centers were simply taking advantage of giveaways. Critics of the White House countered that budget increases failed to reverse the effects of the recession. As economic hard times affected more and more Americans, greater numbers of the "new poor" would begin to qualify for assistance. This trend, critics argued, pointed to the need for more federal involvement rather than less.[31]

In 1983, Democrats in Congress held ranks in budget negotiations to the extent that they blocked further poverty-program cuts and returned a number of domestic programs to their 1981 allocations. Armed with an additional twenty-six seats, House Democrats began to frame hunger as an issue on which they could challenge the president. Speaker of the House Thomas P. O'Neill Jr. suggested that congressional opposition to further poverty-program cuts represented the will of the people, who "believe that Reagan policies are unfair and have gone too far."[32]

House moves to slow the Reagan revolution restored funding to some programs without challenging the basic direction of the administration's retrenchment of welfare. As media attention and public concern with hunger increased, the House of Representatives tried to relax eligibility standards for school lunches, but the Republican-controlled Senate failed to act on the measure.

In 1984, Congress passed the Deficit Reduction Assistance Act, which restored eligibility to some AFDC recipients with independent earnings and raised the eligibility ceiling to 185 percent of the standard of need. The 1984 changes also allowed states to continue Medicaid support for fifteen months after AFDC payments ended. Despite these increases, discretionary spending on social welfare remained below 1981 levels.

Throughout the remainder of the Reagan presidency, the White House held the line on social-services spending. Each year, administration welfare proposals demanded workfare for AFDC recipients, stricter child-support enforcement, and large reductions in energy assistance programs.[33] While Congress rejected proposals to eliminate additional community development programs, it agreed to sharply cut funding to these programs.

Meanwhile, as reports of hunger in America mounted, Congress moved to expand food-stamp eligibility and benefits. More than $520 million were added to food-stamp appropriations in 1985. By the middle of the decade, however, all domestic spending faced the tough scrutiny of a budgeting process increasingly hamstrung by the deficit.[34]

In brief, the two Reagan terms were characterized by a period of intense budget cuts in domestic spending and social services, followed by a long period of level funding that was the result of a budget standoff between the White House and Congress. Gradually a cleavage appeared between the president and Congress over domestic-spending priorities. This divergence first appeared in the wake of the ambiguous 1982 midterm elections and was exacerbated by the economic recession. Despite White House assurances that more money than ever before was being spent on domestic assistance programs, the outcry against budget cuts continued.

Over his eight years of budget making, President Reagan failed to reduce social programs to the extent he had intended. Rather than the 14 percent real decrease in spending on domestic social services projected in his fiscal 1983 budget, actual spending grew by nearly 4 percent a year after inflation. Still, antipoverty advocates complained that Reagan had undermined the social-welfare safety net. Welfare spending grew, they argued, because of recession and entitlement programs, and more and more people lost their jobs or were working for wages that left them below the poverty line. Beyond entitlement programs, the Reagan revolution effectively pruned discretionary spending. "It's hard to imagine [these programs] regaining any significant share of government outlays," argued Robert Greenstein, director of the Center on Budget and Policy Priorities.[35]

THE NEW CLASS WAR: REAGAN AND THE POOR

The political ramifications of the Reagan revolution included growing income inequality. Republican pollster Vincent Breglio grumbled that the Republican party's "biggest fear is that the Democrats surface with a leader who is able to capitalize on the theme of economic populism."[36] Other observers noted the same process of increasing class divisions and tension. *Business Week* commented that "the Great Divide between rich and poor in America . . . is perhaps the most troubling legacy of the 1980s."[37]

Traditionally, overall economic growth has led to gains for the poor. From World War II through the 1970s, there was a positive and steady correlation between overall economic growth and the well-being of the poor.[38] The general economic recovery of the mid-1980s refocused attention on the poor because their condition failed to improve. In 1987, the Physicians' Task Force on Hunger in America noted that "economic growth has come to America. The economy is in its fifty-eighth month of expansion, the unemployment rate is down and the number of new jobs is up. Poverty has fallen somewhat, and the rate of inflation is relatively low. By these indices the national economy is strong and productive. . . . How can it be that the economy is so robust, yet so many American families remain hungry?"[39]

During the course of the Reagan presidency, median family income rose by 7.5 percent while poverty remained high. One effect of this lopsided recovery was the dissipation of any remaining vestiges of middle-class support for a movement for social justice, as middle-income earners generally benefited from economic growth. Paradoxically, despite general economic recovery, U.S. poverty levels at the end of the 1980s were as high as at the start of the War on Poverty nearly thirty years earlier. During the Reagan years, recession, tax cuts, changing welfare laws, and business shifts drove increasing numbers of people into poverty, deprived them of health care, and increased their tax burden.[40]

Government policy contributed directly to changes in the relative security of the rich and poor. The tax cuts enacted between 1977 and 1992 enriched the wealthy, increased the tax burden of the middle class, and grossly inflated the national debt.[41] In effect, tax cuts plus the rising deficit hamstrung the ability of both the federal and state governments to counter growing poverty rates because there was no money left to reinvest in social-service programs. Between 1979 and 1989 the income of the poorest fifth of the country actually decreased by 2.1 percent while that of the next poorest fifth remained virtually unchanged. Meanwhile, the upper middle class gained 10.6 percent in income and the richest fifth of the country experienced income growth of 20.4 percent.[42] A decade of redistribution has meant that the richest 2.5 million Americans, 1 percent of the population, have nearly as much income as the poorest 40 percent of the country.[43] Although increasing the wealth of the rich in society may signal raised well-being of society as a whole, growing income disparity potentially leads to class conflict.

That widening class divisions would lead to open hostility between rich and poor was nervously discussed after the urban riots in the spring of 1992. As President George Bush toured the carnage of South-Central Los Angeles, protesters followed with a twenty-foot banner blaming the damage not on the verdict in the Rodney King case but on twelve years of Reagan-Bush economic policies. Some observers quickly ruled out political interpretations of the insurgency, attributing the riots to indiscriminate violence and gang delinquency.[44] The strongest evidence of a class-based political message in these events is found in middle-class responses, including calls for more police protection, stiffer sentences, and building walls around more affluent suburbs.[45]

3

The Historical Development of
Poverty Advocacy

In the United States, social-welfare policy-making has developed along two paths, one episodic, the other incremental. The reform impulse is strong in welfare policy, directed both toward reducing poverty and social malaise and toward redefining the role of relief efforts. The episodic emergence of reform movements establishes new directions for welfare efforts. In this respect, the settlement house movement, the New Deal, the Great Society, and the Reagan revolution (or New Federalism) were fundamentally similar. American reform movements have shared remarkably consistent underpinnings. Each round of reform mobilization has taken aim at the failures of existing welfare efforts. In subsequent assaults on poverty and welfare, reformers vow to more carefully target the "deserving" poor and promise that effective inducements will move people from the dole to paid-work positions, in turn leading to the withering away of welfare altogether. Each wave of reform is sold to the public as economically viable and, ultimately, as cheaper than existing programs. The Clinton administration welfare-reform package hints at the historical constancy of reform efforts: "History suggests that reforming [welfare] reform will not be an easy task. Many a president before Clinton has come to office promising a receptive public that he will sharply *decrease* both welfare costs and caseloads and the misery attendant thereon."[1]

A second line of development in welfare policy is the incremental process of constructing and revising relief programs. The incremental policy-making process can respond to the external shocks caused by episodic reform movements, particularly when reformers' demands lead to the adoption of new legislation (as occurred with the New Deal, the Great Society, and New Federalism). But importantly, the incremental process continues regardless of the impetus of major society-wide reform efforts. The typical intersection of the two processes occurs when issues are thrust into national attention by reform proponents and are then embraced by the legislature and the White House. Responding to this surge in attention, government programs are created and institutionalized to command a continuing band of resources—including agenda space, budget allocations, and, potentially, expansions. Consequently, advocates face different opportunities and constraints during and between reform movements. During such moments of reform, advocates seek major concessions; after this impulse passes, they work for incremental reallocations and program expansions. Across time, the existence of advocacy organizations will increasingly depend on their ability either to diversify their agendas to capture emerging issues or to take contract income generated from the programs they lobby. In this way, advocates in the hunger lobby evolve with the opportunities created by broader developments in and between reform movements.

Advocacy organizations and their abilities to represent the interests of the poor have consequently emerged and evolved in response to both episodic and incremental facets of social-welfare policy development. The universe of groups, and the set of issues they advance, is prone to dramatic expansion and contraction during the periodic and urgent assaults on welfare that reform efforts represent. At other times, the institutionalized lobbying efforts of advocates can be critical to either expanding or opposing changes proposed during waves of reform. This chapter follows these processes as they led to the development of a national venue for antipoverty advocacy and, in turn, to the creation of the hunger lobby.

The transition from local to national responses to poverty and the parallel development of a national network of public-interest groups pursuing a poor people's agenda followed from a number of historical developments. First, national conceptions of the causes of poverty increasingly shifted from local labor conditions to national economic problems. In response, efforts to fashion appropriate relief efforts also shifted from private and local initiatives to national and federal ones. From the time of the New Deal to the Great Society, the weight of American welfare relief initiatives went from churches and charities to state and national governments.

Second, the organization and operations of reform organizations and relief agencies grew increasingly formal and professionalized as their role in the provision of social services increased. Over the years, federal reforms including the provision of emergency and long-term relief services have increasingly been channeled through government agencies and, in turn, through not-for-profit organizations. This institutionalization has had the effect of creating identifiable and consistent access points for lobbying efforts, as well as formalizing the role of nonprofit organizations and advocates in the welfare policy-making process.

Third, recurrent efforts by political reformers to empower poor communities led to programs that encouraged the creation of political organizations to speak for poor people's interests. These organizations then expanded their organizational positions and political missions in response to their internal agendas and grant opportunities extended by private foundations and the federal government.

RESPONSIBILITY FOR POVERTY RELIEF BEFORE THE GREAT DEPRESSION

The Great Depression marked a turning point in American attitudes toward poverty and welfare. Before the Depression, reformers concentrated on local solutions to poverty, which was thought to arise from local labor conditions or from the lifestyles of the poor.[2] As a community problem, poverty relief was left to local churches and charities. Relief efforts were uneven, geared toward small communities, and local in scope. They included "casual *ad hoc* relief given by churches; the aid given to immigrants by ethnic societies; . . . more widespread, systematic philanthropy . . . [and the more widespread] efforts of the Catholic church."[3]

At a time when towns and villages were small and populations less mobile, relief was primarily provided by local organizations on the basis of community membership.[4] Caring for kith and kin became increasingly problematic, however, as demographic patterns changed when people migrated to larger, more industrialized cities in search of work. With mobility came the dislocation of local support structures, which were overwhelmed by the need created during the Great Depression. The combination of nationwide economic malaise and local government bankruptcy led to more urgent demands for state and federal intervention in poverty, which was increasingly seen as a national rather than a local problem.

The call for comprehensive responses to poverty has historically come from churches, charities, organized labor, and, increasingly, from service-providing organizations, as well as community service and civil-rights organizations.[5] The first nationwide wave of private philanthropies actively providing poverty relief was church based. After 1880, most cities had a Charities Organization Society, which distributed religious tracts and provided emergency relief through their "friendly visits."[6]

A critical difference between these early reformers and their modern counterparts in the hunger lobby concerned their view of government. Unlike modern reformers, the "friendly visitation" societies worked to eliminate government-funded poverty relief, believing that psychological counseling most effectively and efficiently helped the poor. The societies' emphasis on voluntarism became ingrained in welfare relief during the late 1800s, leading to the creation of Social Service Exchanges, Community Chests, and the United Way. Like the United Way, many of these organizations survive and continue the tradition of volunteer service and private relief efforts.[7] They have been tremendously successful at raising contributions nationwide to provide emergency services and to respond quickly to disasters and other emergencies, channeling massive outpourings of public concern for disaster victims. True to their historical roots, these organizations continue to avoid political advocacy, preferring to concentrate on service provision rather than political reform.

A second important predecessor to the hunger lobby was the settlement house movement, which built community-oriented halfway houses in the slum areas of many major cities around the turn of the century.[8] With the assistance of the Salvation Army, these houses provided food and clothing to the most poverty-stricken urban residents.[9] The settlement house movement gained the sponsorship of wealthy individuals and private corporations interested in offering a level of social welfare to quell labor dissent and "improve" the quality of the workforce.[10] As Michael Katz put it, "Welfare capitalism was an attempt to integrate an often hostile, foreign, unstable labor force into the social order by winning the commitment of workers to individual firms and to American capitalism. It involved a number of strategies: establishing model towns'. . . ; raising real wages; promoting home ownership; and introducing pensions and other benefits."[11]

Management's increasing concern with social problems and labor unrest led to the creation of nonreligious service agencies and foundations, which originated through large, private endowments.[12] The heyday for foundation formation was between 1920 and 1931, when the total number of secular and religious foundations grew to nearly 350.[13] With increasing numbers of well-funded relief agencies working to remedy social ills, groups diversified their efforts. Many took their cue from the Charities Organization Societies and shifted from direct relief to psychological casework administered by professional social workers. In this transition, the foundations also began to move from a notion of individual responsibility to a quest for more systemic, pathological reasons underlying the existence of poverty. Growing professionalization also contributed to an increasingly national, universalistic focus on both poverty and welfare relief.[14]

Founded in 1936 "to serve the public welfare through grants for educational, scientific and charitable purposes," the Ford Foundation quickly established its preeminence in public and private welfare reform, granting more than $1.9 billion to colleges, universities, schools, and community organizations between 1950 and 1963.[15] In its funding priorities, the Ford Foundation sought not only to expand available relief services but also to nurture the political and social life of poor communities.[16]

STATE AND FEDERAL INVOLVEMENT IN PROVIDING FOR THE POOR

Government involvement in poverty relief developed alongside private relief agencies. Individual states moved to establish poor laws early in the nineteenth century and soon afterward began to regulate operating conditions and contribute to the budgets of poor houses. In more recent years, the states have come to play an increasing variety of roles in providing relief, including program oversight, outreach, and funding.

Federal involvement in welfare provision began tentatively, with symbolic overtures such as the White House Conference on Children in 1909 and the creation of the Children's Bureau in 1912.[17] The early emphasis on children became a constant in reform movements in the United States. Since before the Depression, reformers have attempted to target deserving subgroups of poor people. Children provided a symbolic as well as tangible target for relief efforts (a target that can seldom be reached outside the context of their families). Yet they provide an unambiguous symbol of the "deserving" poor, a group reformers remain keen on identifying.

As opposed to early and largely symbolic efforts, the first tangible federal antipoverty interventions were launched in response to the Great Depression, which demonstrated that poverty was a profound and national malaise, beyond the scope of state and local initiatives. President Franklin D. Roosevelt responded to this national emergency by expanding federal involvement in social welfare. In his inaugural address, Roosevelt outlined three general aims for the New Deal—relief, recovery, and reform. In ensuing sessions, Congress gave substance to this ideal by authorizing massive, nationwide relief.[18]

New Deal programming originally concentrated on emergency relief but quickly shifted to more publicly acceptable and bureaucratically permanent programs.[19] The underlying themes of New Deal reforms have resurfaced in subsequent reform proposals. New Deal programs aimed to wipe away the failures of past policy by extending much needed assistance to the most deserving groups of poor people, were sold as temporary measures that emphasized work, and were promised to be more cost effective than earlier programs. In New Deal policy, grants and pensions were made available to new groups considered deserving, including veterans, the blind, the elderly poor, and widowed mothers.[20]

A second critical component of New Deal legislation was the insistence that these programs would prime the economy but would themselves be short-lived. Federal involvement in relief efforts was conceived, implemented, and sold to the public as temporary. Rather than disappear, New Deal programs institutionalized federal participation in welfare relief by establishing lasting agencies and programs, including the Federal Emergency Relief Administration and the Social Security Administration.[21] These agencies were staffed in turn by professional social workers trained through the private foundations, entrenching the practices and beliefs of these private agencies in federal programs.[22] Consequently, federal programs were institutionalized through bureaucratic agencies, and social-welfare practices were regularized by the new breed of professional social worker, schooled by the foundations and employed in the Social Security Administration.

Domestic poverty receded from public-policy agendas during the economic expansion during the administrations of Harry Truman and Dwight Eisenhower. Through the 1950s, nationwide economic recovery meant better times for most Americans. But widespread poverty continued to plague large regions of the country—reemerging on the national agenda in the 1960 presidential race. The campaign of John F. Kennedy accused the Eisenhower administration of ignoring the prevalence of hunger in America.[23] By the 1960s, public and media attention to the glaring examples of poverty were difficult to reconcile with notions of the affluent society. The United States appeared able to feed its people many times over, with extra food to export. Spurred on by calls for economic justice from the civil-rights movement and attention to dire poverty in the South and in Appalachia, the Kennedy administration pledged to eliminate structural impediments to economic equality.

In turn, President Lyndon Johnson carried forward the Kennedy agenda, launching the War on Poverty and, in language echoed in the Clinton welfare reforms of 1994, offering a "hand up and not a handout."[24] Believing that poverty and inequality resulted from slow economic growth, an unskilled population, and institutional racism, the administration passed the Economic Opportunity Act (EOA) of 1964, which allocated $1 billion to begin a war against poverty.[25] Through the EOA, the Office of Economic Opportunity (OEO) was created to coordinate welfare relief efforts including job training, education and health programs, and support for the elderly.[26] The War on Poverty proposals directed tax money to the aged, poor, and disabled by establishing new entitlement programs.[27] These programs also seemed to offer a response to black Americans who were demanding more political voice and power.[28]

Paralleling the New Deal, the War on Poverty was envisioned as an effective and targeted intervention that would surgically cut to the heart of the causes behind hunger and poverty in the United States. In light of civil-rights unrest, War on Poverty programs were designed to broaden local bases of power, shifting welfare spending to smaller, community-centered programs better able to target deserving groups and avoid bureaucratic excess.[29] On the logic that New Deal welfare spending had overemphasized national coordination, War on Poverty programs were directed to empower local communities. National programs had proved expensive, distant, bureaucratized, and disempowering.[30] Community Action Programs were offered as a remedy. They would provide "autonomous and self-managed organizations . . . competent to exert political influence on behalf of their own self-interest."[31] The ambiguity of this language left room for the development of a wide array of organizations making claims on CSA money, including various "welfare-rights organizations" of the late 1960s and early 1970s, and provided much of the organizational base for the national welfare-rights movement.[32] In some cases, community-based organizations generated direct political action by local groups of poor people, at least for short periods.[33] Along with their organizing efforts, these groups helped decipher complex federal assistance application forms and increased general awareness of available programs.[34] In time, many of these organizations expanded their missions to include a level of institutional political advocacy. Some undertook educational missions before state and national governments. Others were engaged in outreach programs designed to make more poor people aware of available services. Still other groups contracted to provide research and analysis for federal agencies, such as the LSC, or to oversee federally supported programs such as Head Start and federally subsidized housing.

SOURCES OF FEDERAL MONEY CREATED BY THE WAR ON POVERTY

Expanding the pool of available federal grant money for advocacy organizations concerned with issues of poverty and hunger was probably an unintended outcome of the War on Poverty. One of the earliest sources of federal money for advocates was extended through the Emergency Food and Medical Services Program (EFMS), which encompassed the Ford Foundation's "Gray Areas Project," the President's Council on Juvenile Delinquency, and Labor Department grants for the alleviation of poverty.[35] Although EFMS was short-lived, it was the precursor for the subsequent federal grant programs for advocacy groups.

Created by the OEO and later moved to the CSA, the Community Food

and Nutrition Program (CFNP) was created as a way to bolster low participation rates in federal programs, including food stamps and school lunches. The CFNP authorized federal poverty programs to maintain strong
outreach and advocacy programs, so as to extend emergency services to
qualified recipients. Toward this end, CFNP made grants available to both
national- and state-level advocates. One former employee described the
mission of CFNP as "making sure people got food any way they could get it,
and to make sure they knew what federal programs existed to help them
get food."[36] Early CFNP grantees included the Food Research and Action
Center, the Children's Foundation, and the Community Nutrition Institute.

Federal funding for antipoverty advocacy was also found under the Social Security Act, which authorized research into the causes and alleviation
of poverty. These programs generated information on poverty in America
and funded private research organizations. The Legal Services Corporation, another OEO program, also provided research and advocacy money
for advocates, funding groups such as the Center on Social Welfare Policy
and Law and the Food Research and Action Center.[37]

Groups funded by these federal programs operated both as organizers
of the poor and as representatives of traditional Democratic political
causes. Such federal funding for challengers of local, state, and national
policies quickly met resistance on multiple fronts. The attempt to empower
new constituents ruffled established power brokers such as Chicago
mayor Richard J. Daley.[38] While emerging political groups might demand a
voice, entrenched groups saw few advantages in relinquishing the political
control they enjoyed. At the same time, groups that successfully challenged state and federal program guidelines angered politicians eager to
preserve the status quo.[39]

Throughout President Richard M. Nixon's first term, Great Society programs were expanded incrementally, and OEO programs were maintained.
As Nicholas Lehmann reported, the Department of Health, Education,
and Welfare "pushed forward with many school-desegregation cases in
the South. Labor established the use of numerical goals in affirmative action plans. Nixon signed into law . . . a program to create temporary jobs
in the ghettos, a subsidized housing program, revenue sharing and block
grants for cities, increases in welfare payments, and a major expansion of
the food-stamps program."[40] President Nixon also extended Social Security payments to the disabled and considered a guaranteed-minimum-in-
come program.

Many of these program expansions came in the form of "sweeteners" offered to the states in return for acceptance of Nixon's "New Federalism" block grants.[41] In this sense, expansions emerged despite the attempt to cut programs.

Fifty years of growth in federal involvement in welfare provision faced its first serious attack during Nixon's second term. Despite expanded social services, poverty continued to grow, bringing the call for new interventions. Following a recognized pattern of attacking welfare, Nixon was determined to abolish the "failed programs of the past." A few days after reelection, he instructed his staff to "flush [the Model Cities program] . . . OEO—legal services. . . . Take the heat on OEO—it's the right thing to do. Be prepared to take it head on; and flush Model Cities and Great Society. It's failed. Do it, don't say it."[42] But the Nixon administration's attempts to cut domestic spending through block grants had the opposite effect. By adding "sweeteners" to pass the legislation through Congress, the Nixon White House actually orchestrated a rapid expansion in welfare spending.

Despite early boosts through "economic stimulus programs," the administration of President Jimmy Carter also slowed social-welfare spending in response to depleted coffers, national rumblings over tax reform, and concerns with welfare abuse.[43] During the 1970s, the General Accounting Office began to audit tax-exempt organizations providing advocacy on behalf of the poor. The Food Research and Action Center, for example, was audited in 1979 for engaging in excessive political activity, signaling cooling relations between the national government and the poverty advocacy community.[44] Entering the 1980s, a new set of demands were placed on the hunger lobby. Public disenchantment with government management of the economy and welfare was growing and found a voice in the Reagan campaign, leading to heightened tensions with social-justice organizations in the United States.

MOBILIZATION BY PROXY: PUBLIC-INTEREST GROUPS FOR THE POOR

Recognizing the realities of the American political system, which is built largely on the competition between private interest groups, War on Poverty reformers nurtured the development of organizations of public-interest representatives fighting for a poor peoples' agenda. Such nurturing of formal interest groups to support the interests of a silent constituency was at once a bold and questionable move. There is an inevitable friction between marginalized constituencies and middle-class reformers. These public-interest groups could count on little involvement or support from the constituency they worked to represent.

To understand the successes and failures of these organizations over the

1980s, it is necessary to view them as political interest groups. What are the advantages and disadvantages of public-interest groups as poverty fighters? The infusion of public and private funding and growing government involvement in poverty advocacy generated a strange creature: the public-interest poverty fighter. Interest groups are unlikely heroes in the fight against poverty. In general, interest groups are private, nongovernmental organizations that advance the collective agenda of their members. Political interest groups actively participate in modern democratic politics. Despite increased regulation, including formal registration requirements and strict guidelines governing the political activity of tax-exempt organizations, American politics has seen an explosion in the number of interest groups over the last thirty years.[45] The reasons behind this explosion include heightened public awareness of political issues and concerns, increased federal involvement in state politics, and increasingly sophisticated techniques for enlisting members and patrons.[46] Each of these changes created new opportunities and expanded needs for private sources of representation. Evaluations of the role played by interest groups, however, range from the malevolent to the benign.[47]

Interest groups have been called the "feature of political power most characteristic of American democracy" both because they have long been active in politics in this country and because they give voice to the American tendency to coalesce in groups, as noted by Alexis de Tocqueville in 1831:[48] "Americans of all ages, all stations in life, and all types of dispositions are forever forming associations . . . religious, moral, serious, futile, very general and very limited, immensely large and very minute. Americans combine great individualism with an attitude toward community action that knows no counterpart in the world."[49] Some observers, following Tocqueville, have interpreted interest groups as the inevitable outcome of American inclinations to coalesce. Writing in 1908, Arthur Bentley dismissed concerns over insidious and cloaked interest-group power, arguing that groups were best compared to the songs sung by armies as they marched into battle. As with battle hymns, Bentley argued, political interest groups were simply a manifestation of the popular wave of support that carried them along and had as little independent effect on the outcome of politics as do songs in battle—both merely served to rally and lift the spirits of the troops.[50]

Evaluations of the role of private interests in American politics have often been more condemnatory. James Madison called the exercise of power by private groups "the most serious problem to be faced by popular government."[51] Echoing Madison, leaders of the Progressive movement expressed concerns over the bonds between special interests and corrupt politicians and argued that interest groups wielded excessive political power in the American system.[52] Contemporary debates about political corruption again focus on the power and representativeness of interest groups and on the types of interests they promote. In a system that relies on a detachment between groups petitioning government and political decision makers, the presence of "cozy triangles" and "issue networks" that link the interests of elected officials, executive agencies, and political interest groups poses a serious threat to the public interest.[53]

FIGHTING FOR THE HUNGRY: PUBLIC-INTEREST GROUPS FOR SOCIAL JUSTICE

As we have seen, notions of responsibility for poverty relief shifted after the New Deal from the private to public and from the local to the national level. This shift precipitated a change in the nature of private political advocacy associations as well. The increasing sweep of national politics since the New Deal made Washington central to many facets of policy-making and, in turn, spurred the growth of national advocacy groups. These changes were part of a larger evolution in the nature of political-interest groups and public interest representation in America.

In the 1950s, David Truman argued that political interest groups were central to democratic political systems because they crystalized the latent competition between small, otherwise silent groups.[54] In effect, Truman speculated, the sum of the conflicts between various private groups was the secret to effective democratic governance. Good government, therefore, not only allowed groups to exist but also paid attention to their demands and remained alert to the size and arguments of various representative organizations.

Competition among interest groups, mediated by a sage and impartial state, produces policies that are more or less aligned with public desires. In Truman's words, "The group system is . . . an accurate indicator of politically relevant social interests, as well as a reliable channel of representation distinct from parties and elections."[55] This interaction between groups both allows for participation and guards against its excesses.[56] Reformers who work to create political organizations by and for the poor accept the basic premise that group representation is a worthwhile endeavor in contemporary politics. They seek, however, to create groups where there is little "natural tendency" for them to form, believing that the very existence of representative organizations for marginalized people makes their representation and participation more likely.

Public interest advocates are among the fastest-growing segments of the interest-group realm, fighting for broad aspects of the "public interest."[57] Groups with agendas as diverse as the American Civil Liberties Union (ACLU) and the Religious Roundtable fall into this category—seeking to promote their own notion of society's "general welfare" rather than secure specific, material benefits for their members.[58] Unlike professional associations and economically oriented groups, which seek benefits for small and clearly defined populations, public-interest groups pursue nonexcludable benefits. An environmental group pursuing a ban on seal pelt imports, for example, returns to members and nonmembers alike the protection of the seal pups.[59]

Organizational problems plague groups offering only collective benefits. (For example, if wilderness protection is already in good hands, what would motivate *my* contribution to the cause?) An individual concerned about the environment and aware of the work done by the Sierra Club or Greenpeace may become complacent, believing environmental groups are engaged in the fight. For this reason, public-interest groups are susceptible to "free riders," who enjoy the gains made by the group without contributing to the collective effort.[60] Because they are liable to collapse under the weight of free riders, public-interest groups are highly dependent on patrons for support. In the United States, therefore, their number and diversity varies in response to structural opportunities extended by foundation and corporate philanthropy and government grants.[61]

Government grants fund a wide range of private advocacy groups. At its best, this patronage allows groups to form that would never otherwise be heard—particularly marginalized, resource-poor, and geographically dispersed groups, such as farmers, that would be unlikely to coalesce without such funding. This logic underlay the formation of the American Farm Bureau Federation, for example. Today, federally funded groups actively participate in policy-making arenas ranging from banking to the environment. In practice, government grants for outreach or advocacy have usually gone to the organizations best positioned to apply for them. While government largess may bring new voices into politics, most federally supported advocacy reflects contours of the pressure system at large. As a result, business and professional groups, as well as state and local governments, have been the principal benefactors of federal funding during both Democratic and Republican presidential administrations.[62] In this respect, federal funding entrenches rather than expands existing patterns of interest representation. Consequently, government support ensures private involvement in policy-making but not a broader base of interest-group representation.

POVERTY ADVOCATES AS POLITICAL INTEREST GROUPS

Public-interest groups advocating on behalf of the poor face the same organizational constraints as other public-interest groups, but their existence is particularly precarious because they tend to rely heavily on a small group of funders centered on the federal government. Federal funding has traditionally been thought to shield organizations from the constant pressure to raise funds while imposing programmatic constraints on their activities.[63]

As they depend more and more on institutional support, public-interest groups grow increasingly reliant on fewer funders, making their formation and maintenance the result of institutional sanction rather than a response to groundswells of popular protest.[64] Likewise, any defections among a handful of funders may jeopardize a group's existence. Institutional funding seriously constrains the resources and political avenues available to groups.[65] Grant recipients may receive explicit or implied instructions about the types of action, including tactics and political goals, that are acceptable to funders.[66]

These general tendencies were evident in the events of the 1980s, which proved to be a period of turmoil for private foundations committed to social services. Commenting on the national mood and philanthropic priorities during the 1980s, the Ford Foundation noted:

> at the start of this decade . . . the climate in America suggested a retreat from earlier commitments to fighting poverty and championing equal rights and civil liberties. Inflation was high, and the nation seemed to have suffered a loss of faith in its own future. Along with this anxiety about what lay ahead, there seemed to be a withering of the country's spirit of generosity, a growing unwillingness to help the least fortunate. And across the world many nations seemed more intent on building walls around their privilege than joining together to solve common problems.[67]

Faced by reduced federal spending, the private sector's ability to respond was overwhelmed by the magnitude of increased need. According to the Ford Foundation's 1982 annual report: "demands for Foundation support have been increasing as national priorities and strategies have left many organizations and the social, cultural, and educational issues they address without adequate funding. We have tried to be responsive to this need. But when foundation and corporate philanthropic spending together amount to less than $6 billion per year, much of which is committed to important ongoing activities, it is impossible to compensate significantly for the withdrawal or reduction of federal support in amounts many times greater."[68]

Advocacy groups scrambled to find new sources of income when the federal government curtailed its support.[69] The capacities of private foundations, however, were overwhelmed by the magnitude of lost income from federal grants. Not only were foundations unable to simply underwrite the Reagan retrenchment, but changes in tax laws made foundations increasingly wary of associating with political activists in the hunger lobby.[70] Charitable foundations feared attacks on their tax-exempt status for associating with unpopular political interest groups. For some foundations, inflation-ravaged endowments and apparent public support for the Reagan cuts meant that antipoverty groups were off-limits. One foundation executive, recounting the panic among advocates in the early 1980s, explained that the foundations simply could not afford to get involved.[71]

Over the longer term, social-justice advocates found themselves competing with other emerging concerns as well as with other groups within their own issue sector. Much private giving went to direct-service providers, who reported "dramatic and sometimes even stunning" increases of 50 to 500 percent in demand for their services.[72] Most private dollars were directed toward service providers and emergency relief organizations rather than toward groups advocating political change. The largest single private contributor to social services in the United States remains the United Way. By 1985, virtually one quarter of all giving to social services came from the United Way, implicitly favoring organizations with certain agendas and methods while marginalizing almost all groups with explicitly political rather than service-oriented missions.

From the initiation of the War on Poverty programs until the reductions effected by the OBRA of the early 1980s, the federal government was the primary source of support for a range of antipoverty organizations including community-development corporations, community-services agencies, and legal-services back-up centers. When federal funding was cut off, poverty advocates found themselves in extremely uncertain organizational and political positions.

When private foundations and the federal government are the principal sources of funding for an entire sector of interest organizations, they exert a powerful influence on the voices heard in policy-making. This process may tip the ideological balance of interests represented on any particular public-policy issue. The Reagan revolution did not decrease the number of lobbyists in the nation's capital; during the 1980s, the number of interest groups in Washington rose rapidly. But a marked shift occurred in the types of groups gaining policy access and cooperation from federal agencies.[73] Hundreds of millions of dollars in federal grant money remained available to not-for-profit groups, but most of this money was earmarked for groups sympathetic to the Reagan agenda.[74] Groups interested in social-welfare policy were shut out of policy-making and complained of dwindling access and cooperation.[75]

4

Public-Interest-Group Responses

Decreased federal investment in social services during economic recession, coupled with less funding for poverty advocacy, suggests two different responses.[1] Dramatic cuts in social services would likely lead to a countermobilization by concerned organizations and individuals, spurred to action by this political assault and policy crisis. After all, maintaining and increasing federal involvement in welfare provision and poverty alleviation had been the principal agenda item of the hunger lobby. A political mobilization in response to policy shifts on social justice would have paralleled other movements of the 1980s. Environmental groups, for example, gained increased membership and mounted a countermobilization in response to the anticonservation stance of Secretary of the Interior James Watt. Acknowledging the effect of a powerful antagonist on a political movement, the Sierra Club credited Watt and President Reagan as superior fund-raisers for the club.[2] Following the same pattern, advocates for the poor had every reason to mobilize as the administration retreated from social-welfare provision.

At the same time, however, budget cuts gutted the hunger lobby. The loss of a primary source of income for an entire sector of public-interest groups is almost unprecedented, and its effects are not only difficult to judge but also critical to understanding how representation takes place on public-policy issues in the United States. Massive funding cuts have the potential to crush the possibilities for mobilization, diverting representative organizations from political action in their scramble to remain viable.

What is the combined effect of policy crisis and resource constraints on public-interest-group representation? Does the withdrawal of a major funding source have the same effect on an advocacy community as the withdrawal of a factory can have on a small town? What effect do cuts in federal grants have on an already-volatile sector of advocacy groups? Were

Table 1. Chronological Listing of Social-Justice Organizations Providing Advocacy on Domestic Poverty Issues

Center on Social Welfare Policy and Law	1965
Center for Community Change	1968
National Association for the Southern Poor	1968
Center for Law and Social Policy	1969
Children's Foundation	1969
Community for Creative Non-Violence	1970
Community Nutrition Institute	1970
Food Research and Action Center	1970
Association of Community Organizations for Reform Now (ACORN)	1970
Partnership for Democracy	1970
Children's Defense Fund	1973
Bread for the World	1975
Interreligious Taskforce on U.S. Food Policy (Interfaith Action/Interfaith IMPACT)	1975
Working Group on Domestic Hunger & Poverty	1975
National Low Income Housing Coalition	1978
Center on Budget and Policy Priorities	1981
RESULTS	1981
National Community Action Foundation	1981
National Coalition for the Homeless	1982
Public Voice for Food and Health Policy	1982
National Alliance to End Homelessness	1983
Physician's Task force on Hunger in America	1984
National Union for the Homeless	1986
National Law Center on Homelessness and Poverty	1989
Housing Works Inc.	1991
Homes Not Jails	1993

Note: The principal agenda items for these organizations include advocacy, community development, children's welfare, poverty, hunger and homelessness.

antipoverty groups able to withstand this assault, or did they retrench organizationally and become politically silent? Can we identify marked differences between the activities of groups hard hit by budget cuts and those that escaped the ax? One way to address these questions is by looking at patterns of group formation. Public-interest groups are generally short-lived, emerging and fading with concern over particular policy issues.[3] Short life expectancies mean that public-interest group sectors are susceptible to quick depletion if new groups do not continue to form to replace organizations on the wane.

Table 1 presents a chronological listing of antipoverty organizations founded since the War on Poverty and active today.[4] Most of these organizations offer a combination of emergency services and political action.

Their variety indicates the range of niches filled by antipoverty groups. The founding dates of organizations in table 1 correspond with contemporary waves of advocacy-group development, in response to OEO, LSC, CSA, and private foundation grants in the 1960s and 1970s and to income from private grants directed toward their efforts arising from the political events of the 1980s.

The political organizations included in table 1 represent a long-term evolution of advocates responding to the social and political changes initiated during the New Deal era and continued and expanded through the Great Society. As the table indicates, most contemporary antipoverty groups were formed in the decade between 1965 and 1975, coinciding with expanded federal initiatives offered through the Great Society for the development of community-based groups. Furthermore, each period of group formation corresponds with particular types of groups. For example, corresponding with the welfare-rights movement, the period between 1966 and 1975 saw the emergence of legal-services centers such as the Food Research and Action Center (FRAC) and the Center on Social Welfare Policy and Law (CSWPL).

A second wave of group formation is evident since 1980. Table 1 indicates a rejuvenation of this group sector in response to the Reagan agenda and the emergence of the homeless movement, as six new groups were formed during the first Reagan term and a seventh group, the National Union for the Homeless, was formed during the second Reagan term. Most recently, emerging groups have focused their energies locally, contesting local anti-panhandling restrictions and bans on public sleeping, for example.[5]

TURNOVER RATES OF ADVOCACY GROUPS

New antipoverty groups have historically emerged in response to social and political trends, including the New Deal, the Great Society, and the Reagan retrenchment. While new groups continued to form through the 1980s, we are left to wonder how effective these groups have been. New groups, after all, are scrambling to establish organizational footholds. This is particularly true for public-interest groups, which have emerged increasingly rapidly but also have the shortest life expectancy of any political interest group.[6] We would expect both tendencies to have been exacerbated during the 1980s, responding to White House shifts in domestic policy.[7]

Over the decade, the total number of political interest groups, including antipoverty advocates, increased.[8] On the basis of aggregate numbers, the total number of groups in the hunger lobby seems to have remained constant despite resource contraction. In fact, this period of turbulence escalated the rate of growth of the interest-group realm. For the hunger lobby, new groups formed in response to the rediscovery of poverty in the form of homelessness and Third World famine, emerging policy agendas, and shifting movement "frames," such as welfare rights, White House mean spiritedness, and homelessness.[9]

LINKS BETWEEN ADVOCACY GROUPS AND THE POOR

Public interest-groups and social-movement organizations often claim to speak for a concerned and large membership. These groups, therefore, are inclined to identify themselves as membership groups even if they only tangentially rely on members. This characterizes many of the organizations within the hunger lobby.

The links between advocacy groups and poor people are tentative. Most groups offer some kind of free or reduced-priced membership to the disadvantaged to encourage their participation. A number of organizations actively encourage a level of poor people's involvement in group decision making. For example, FRAC includes present and former recipients of federal assistance on its board of directors.

For the most part, however, antipoverty representation is undertaken by nonmembership groups. Most advocacy organizations receive the large majority of their income from private contributions, grants, and contracts. In this respect advocates are linked to and constrained by institutional funders. Even membership groups usually are disproportionately reliant on a small number of institutional members. The Interfaith Hunger Appeal (IHA), for example, characterizes itself as a membership organization with four sponsoring members: Catholic Relief Services, Church World Service, Lutheran World Relief, and the American Jewish Joint Distribution Committee. These organizations financially support IHA and hold twelve of fourteen positions on the IHA board of trustees. The activities of IHA are further channeled because it also has a grant from the federal Agency for International Development to produce educational seminars and publications.[10]

ADVOCATES IN A POLICY CONTEXT

Having identified a number of periods in which groups formed and certain organizational characteristics, we have evidence of movement within the hunger lobby in response to changes in national policy during the 1980s. After all, eleven of the twenty-six groups formed since 1965 formed in the wake of the 1980 presidential election. What can we say about the organizational position and political action of these groups in response to the Reagan agenda? To augment this overview, we can follow the actions of sample groups over the 1980s.

The six public-interest groups chosen as case studies for this project represent the major strains of active organizations. All these groups share a national focus on policy-making, and they all earned strong reputations both within the advocacy community and from congressional staff members for their advocacy during the domestic policy battles of the 1980s.[11]

These six groups include CSWPL, FRAC, the Community Nutrition Institute (CNI), Bread for the World (BFW), the Center on Budget and Policy Priorities (CBPP), and the Children's Defense Fund (CDF). These six political organizations shared a national focus, maintained offices in Washington DC, and listed advocacy for poor people as their central political concern. In pursuit of their agendas, all six groups prioritized similar types of political action, including contacting members of Congress, drafting legislation, connecting representatives with grass-roots constituencies, and delivering testimony before congressional committees. Through both their existence and political action, these groups provided to the very poor the type of representation thought to be available only to the profoundly wealthy.

At the same time, the cases vary across important dimensions, including their relation with the federal government and, consequently, their resource levels throughout the decade, their specific issue domains, and their strategies for maintaining their organizations and taking political action.

The six case studies are listed in table 2, categorized by their principal funding sources over the 1980s as well as their programmatic focus and founding dates. Five of these groups emerged in response to the War on Poverty and the concurrent wave of recognition of the continuing prevalence of hunger and poverty in the United States. The sixth group, the CBPP, represents a second wave of poverty activists, organized to combat both the conservative backlash against poverty programs and liberal support structures.

Their reputations as some of the most effective, connected, and active groups in the hunger lobby make these cases interesting for study, as they appear to have been able to respond to policy crisis and to remain active participants in pressure politics. These cases also allow us to measure the importance of budget continuity for group activity because these groups split across the critical dimension of resource maintenance.

Three of the cases relied heavily on income from federal grants and consequently had constructed operating agendas linked closely with governmental agencies and federal action. These three groups subsequently

Table 2. Six Case Studies:
National Advocacy Groups, Their Principal Funding Sources, Programmatic Focus, and Founding Dates

Group	Principal External Funding Sources	Programmatic Focus	Year Founded
Bread for the World	Individual and institutional members and private foundation grants	Domestic and international hunger and poverty	1975
Center on Budget and Policy Priorities	Foundation grants	Analysis of federal spending priorities on social welfare	1981
Center on Social Welfare Policy and Law	Legal Services Corporation, private foundations	Means-tested cash assistance programs	1965
Children's Defense Fund	Private individual and foundation grants	Health and welfare of children, especially children in poverty	1973
Community Nutrition Institute	Individual and institutional member dues	Federal food assistance programs	1970
Food Research and Action Center	Legal Services Corporation, individual and foundation grants	Federal food assistance programs	1970

found themselves scrambling to generate replacement income in order to remain in existence. The other three case studies were privately funded and, partly in response to this organizational situation, adopted a more directly oppositional stance to government action. Given their relative isolation from budget cuts, privately funded groups did not suffer directly from withdrawn federal income. Still, these groups felt the pinch of increased competition for private funding, as well as constricting access to decision makers. In the words of a CBPP representative: "We have never had government funding. . . . We don't feel it is something we want, given our fundamental criticisms of government policies. We have always relied entirely on foundation grants. As a result, we have never had to deal with the issue of having to replace funding."[12]

Marian Wright Edelman, founder of CDF, expressed a similar sentiment: "I decided long ago never to take a government dollar, and I have never been so happy in my life at a decision . . . but I am deeply concerned that the fallout from cuts in other group's budgets will be increased responsibilities on organizations such as ours."[13]

Given their shared political agendas and differing funding histories, these six groups offer the possibility of evaluating the strategic actions of representative advocacy organizations across the critical dimension of resource stability.

A METHOD FOR COMPARING PUBLIC-INTEREST GROUPS

The basis of my evaluation of these organizations is a set of interviews conducted with current and former organizational directors, officers, and staff members between 1989 and 1994. I contacted representatives for each group several times over this five-year period in order to augment and reassess their continuing activities since 1980. I also interviewed antipoverty and hunger activists associated with other advocacy groups at the national and state levels and House of Representatives staff members who worked closely with the former Select Committee on Hunger. The combined responses from these interviews are augmented by an extensive set of organizational documents, including annual reports and financial statements—a source underutilized by political scientists. In fact, as this project evolved, the objective record provided by financial documents provided the basis for ongoing discussions with organizational representatives. Budget information would indicate shifting priorities and allocation decisions of each group, which I was able to assess both as objective measures of political context *and* as explained by group representatives.

Each group granted me access to its Internal Revenue Service (IRS) 990 forms, as well as audited financial statements or comparable sources of budget information for each year in question. These income figures allow for comparative analysis of advocates' funding and expenditures.[14]

The combination of personal interviews and financial information not only allows us to paint a picture of fundamental aspects of group health and organizational and political decisions but also fleshes out such an analysis with the additional benefit of the insights, observations, and explanations offered by group representatives. These measures of organizational and strategic decisions are then compared with a second, externally generated, measure of political action. In both their printed material and in interviews, group representatives stressed the importance their organizations ascribed to participation in the congressional hearing process. Their levels of testimony delivery therefore offer a useful corroborating measure of political action, indicative of their health and activity.[15]

While selected cases allow for systematic data collection from representative organizations, a number of limitations are also imposed on the study by the choice of cases. In this investigation, two of these limitations deserve specific mention. First, all these organizations are explicitly national in focus; furthermore, for reasons discussed below, BFW increasingly turned to international events. This mixed focus makes it difficult to generalize from these cases to the organizational and political situation of regional and local organizations, which are important components of the American system of service delivery and political representation. A second limitation of this selection is that all of these groups are advocates; that is, they are interested in political change and system-level responses to poverty and hunger. By design, this selection excludes organizations that are principally service providers such as food banks and soup kitchens, many of which have worked vigorously to combat hunger in America and which provide a second layer of organizational infrastructure for collective action by and for the poor.[16] Both of these exclusions follow from my principal research questions about the political voice of the poor in national politics during the 1980s.

ORGANIZATIONAL CHARACTERISTICS OF SOCIAL-JUSTICE ADVOCACY GROUPS

Founded in 1965 by the LSC, the CSWPL develops analyses for legal-services lawyers, welfare groups, Congress, interest groups, and private individuals. The CSWPL's primary concern is with means-tested cash public-assistance programs, including AFDC, SSI, and state and local general assistance programs. The CSWPL remains the only national legal and policy organization dealing exclusively with these programs.[17] Through this agenda, it concentrates on the least popular and most debated aspects of federal welfare assistance. The CSWPL emerged as an early leader among groups in the hunger lobby. Its efforts on behalf of the welfare-rights movement through the late 1960s and early 1970s contributed to the expanding judicial recognition of welfare rights.[18]

Like CSWPL, the FRAC is also known for its ability to compel agency compliance with judicial rulings.[19] Founded in 1970, FRAC provides legal research and national-level advocacy for the nation's network of food banks, soup kitchens, and local and state departments of social services, serving as an umbrella organization for both publicly and privately funded service providers. In addition, FRAC conducts educational and training programs on the problems of hunger and poverty for constituent groups, federal agencies, and congressional staff.[20]

The CNI was also founded in 1970, taking advantage of federal funding opportunities made available through Great Society programs. It was awarded one of the first CFNP grants to make information on federal food programs more accessible to potential recipients. Through the early 1980s, CNI lobbied on food and nutrition issues, including hunger, food quality and safety, nutrition research, food programs, and education. The organization's stated objective was securing a food system that "sustains cultural and social values and maintains human health."[21]

The remaining three cases considered here shared similar programmatic agendas yet differed from CSWPL, FRAC, and CNI by explicitly shunning federal funding. Consequently, they received no federal grants and maintained agendas independent from the federal government.

Founded in 1973 as a membership organization, BFW lobbies on domestic and Third World hunger and poverty.[22] On the domestic front, BFW seeks expansions to food and nutrition programs through national information campaigns targeting grass-roots participants and members of Congress. The group believes these efforts help to change congressional perceptions of public sentiment.[23]

A second privately funded group, CBPP, was founded in 1981 by Robert Greenstein, former director of the federal food-stamp program, with an initial major grant from the Field Foundation.[24] Greenstein's departure marked an abrupt shift in the federal food-stamp program from a focus on eliminating hunger toward an emphasis on eliminating food-stamp abuse. Greenstein positioned the fledgling CBPP in direct opposition to the social-welfare priorities of the Reagan administration, regularly challenging the Office of Management and Budget (OMB) analysis of poverty and malnutrition in the United States and the effectiveness of food and hunger programs through position papers distributed to members of Congress, the media, and a network of interested private groups.[25]

Finally, the CDF was founded in 1973 as a nonmembership organization drawing income from major foundation grants. The political activities of CDF are concentrated in child welfare and child health. To this end, it engages in research, public education, monitoring federal agencies, litigating, drafting legislation, and delivering testimony. In addition, CDF assists state and local groups and supports community organizations concerned with child welfare and health, adolescent pregnancy prevention, child care, family services, and child mental health.

The political objectives of the CDF include creating and expanding programs and services, enforcing civil-rights laws, working on program accountability, and increasing parent and community involvement in legislative and administrative decision making. As part of its outreach and educational efforts, the group publishes a number of reports, papers, and a bimonthly newsletter.[26]

The CDF pursues a vigorous and wide-ranging set of antipoverty measures under a far-reaching children's agenda. By focusing on children, CDF avoids some of the problems of definition and self-identification faced by other groups. The group's claim to speak for children has been much more widely accepted than other groups' claims to represent the poor and homeless.[27]

RESOURCES: BUDGETS AND INCOME SOURCES

Drawing from interview responses and the financial information provided by these six organizations, we can construct an overview of their shifting resource levels over the 1980s in the face of marked fluctuations in both federal and private funds. What happened to the income of these groups during the Reagan years? Where did their operating revenue come from? What changes occurred in the sources and amounts of income available to advocates over the decade?

As table 3 indicates, income for the hunger lobby came from government grants (principally from the CSA and the LSC) and from direct public support (including grants from individuals, corporations, and foundations and membership dues). Groups also raise funds themselves through selling publications and running conferences, investments and interest payments, and miscellaneous sources including, for example, the sublease of office space.

Sources of interest-group support establish limits on group action. Con-

Table 3. Annual Income and Percent of Total Income from Government Grants and Private Contributions to Groups Federally Funded in 1980 and to Privately Funded Groups, 1981–1988

	Federally Funded in 1980			*Privately Funded in 1980*		
	CSWPL	FRAC	CNI	BFW	CBPP	CDF
1981 income ($)*	842,981	832,626	1,377,907	1,230,018	193,524	1,937,018
1985 income ($)*	711,781	545,100	263,379	1,741,030	646,400	3,096,719
1988 income ($)*	604,545	686,724	256,130	1,911,395	1,369,278	4,409,104
Percentage changes in total income:						
1981–1985	–18.4	–47.3	–80.9	+41.5	+334.0	+37.4
1985–1988	–17.7	+21.5	–2.8	+9.8	+112.0	+42.2
Change in percentage of total from government:						
Grants, 1981–1985	–18.3	–65.5	–53.6†	0.0	0.0	0.0
Grants, 1985–1988	+1.9	–1.2	–26.4	0.0	0.0	0.0
Change in percentage of total from private funds:						
1981–1985	+21.8	+66.0	+53.6†	+0.2	–4.3	+6.2
1985–1988	–1.9	–4.2	–52.3	+5.5	–1.1	–4.3

*All figures are given in constant 1980 dollars.
†Estimates based on contracts, workshops, subscriptions, and other contributions entries in audited financial statements.
Sources: IRS 990 forms, audited financial statements, and annual reports.

sequently, the number and type of available funders can determine how vigorously advocates will respond to political threats. Further, where a single source provides nearly all of a group's income, turmoil follows from any change in this patronage relation. In a 1981 comparison, citizens groups (such as those in the hunger lobby) were found to draw income from broader support bases than either trade associations or unions.[28] Not all citizens groups, however, have been able to entrench broad bases of support. An examination of group income over the early 1980s found that social-service organizations and the nonprofit sector were hardest hit by reductions in federal grants and contracts.[29]

This sector turmoil is also evident in table 3, which indicates two striking trends in the shifting resource situation facing the hunger lobby. Available federal grant money fell by more than 58 percent between 1981 and 1985 while private funds rose by nearly 75 percent.[30] These trends indicate the dramatic shift in the sources of income available to poverty advocates. During the first Reagan term, federal grant recipients were undercut. The cswpl lost 18 percent of total income, frac lost 32 percent, and cni suffered a devastating 80 percent cut.

Responding to governmental reductions and policy needs, private funders moved to expand their presence in this interest sector. Groups already receiving private grant income disproportionately benefited from expanded foundation and private grant opportunities since they had already established relations with private funders, invested in grantsmanship and fund-raising, and shaped their political agendas in alignment with the foundations. The effects of this advantageous position are evident in the expanding incomes and expenditures of privately funded groups in the sample. The income of bfw rose by more than 40 percent between 1980 and 1985, while the cbpp's income tripled and the cdf surged by 37 percent over the same period.

From the changing budget figures presented in table 3 we see that groups relying on federal support subsequently had a difficult time making the shift to private funding. This transition is difficult in part because it requires groups to gear up for fund-raising and often means they must align their agenda priorities with those of potential funders.[31] Consequently, while groups already receiving private grant income benefited greatly from the expansion of private resources, their federally funded counterparts contracted.

All three of the private groups continued to grow over the decade. Meanwhile, federal grant recipients spent the rest of the decade scrambling to recover. Both the cswpl and the frac redefined their portfolios to prune costs and sought substitutes for lost income. Facing more critical funding loss, the cni enacted deep and lasting organizational retrenchments and concentrated on cost-effective member services.[32]

A closer look at the budgets of these groups across the decade allows us to assess their general organizational trajectory. The cswpl began the second Reagan term with 18.4 percent less income than at the beginning of the decade. During the 1981 budget reconciliation process the group sustained a 31 percent income reduction and subsequently scaled back its organization and supplemented its income with private money.

While federal contributions fell, government grants continued to provide more than 70 percent of cswpl's total income through 1985. At the same time, private contributions increased noticeably (up 21.8 percent between 1981 and 1985). In two different years, direct public support contributed more than 20 percent of the group's income, averting its financial ruin, but private grants were difficult to raise, contributing almost nothing to the organization's budget before 1983. All other income sources the group might have used, including interest and investment income or income generated by staff-run programs, remained negligible. Group income continued to fall (in inflation-adjusted dollars) through 1988. In fact, during the second Reagan term, total group income fell by an additional 17.7 percent. These income reductions forced the group to rethink its political mission, which we will consider in our analysis of group-allocation patterns. In brief, according to a group representative, cswpl was anxious to maintain its funding and programmatic relation with the lsc and, consequently, to escape the administration's wrath. Avoiding further swings of the budget ax meant redirecting efforts away from high-profile lobbying and efforts to undermine White House policy initiatives.[33]

The second federally funded group, frac, handled reduced federal income differently, dramatically shifting its reliance from federal to private grants. Because frac had their csa contract in hand before the 1981 cuts were enacted, it was granted, in effect, a one-year probation to seek out new grants and contracts. The budget ax fell in 1982, however, putting the organization through what one staffer described as "the wrenching transition to private money."[34] From a 1981 high of $832,626, frac, budget plummeted by 35.9 percent in one year. By 1985, the group's income had climbed back to $565,100; still less than 68 percent of the 1981 level. As with the cswpl, 1985 totals reflect an incomplete recovery from the 1981 budget cuts. This gradual recovery continued between 1985 and 1988, as total group income rebounded by 21.5 percent.

As table 3 indicates, federal contributions to frac fell by 65 percent between 1981 and 1985. Meanwhile, direct public support rose by 66 percent. From a 12.7 percent contribution, private grants increased to provide more than 75 percent of total funding for the group between 1983 and 1985. Still other income was generated by raiding the group's endowment and subleasing office space. This organizational retrenchment proved a mixed blessing, adding income but reducing frac's own facilities and resources (reflected in a 50 percent reduction in staff between 1981 and 1982).

The cni suffered an even more dramatic loss of income and barely stayed afloat for much of the decade.[35] From a total budget of $1,377,907 in 1981, income fell by over 80 percent by 1984 to $263,397. Through federal budget cuts, cni lost almost 65 percent of its total income in 1982 alone. According to the group's accounting firm, this combination of income loss and outstanding debt left the organization on the brink of collapse: "the Company may be unable to continue in existence."[36]

In comparison, the 1980s were a period of expansion for the three privately funded groups in the sample. Bread for the World, for example, drew on individual and institutional members to increase its income by more than 41 percent between 1980 and 1985. Between 1985 and 1988, total group income rose by an additional 10 percent. Over the decade, 85 percent of total income was contributed by individual and group members. The nature of these private contributions offers insights into the group's evolving programmatic agenda. Although BFW is a membership organization, only 35 percent of its total income was generated through general member dues. The remaining 65 percent of total income came from member contributions over and above dues. Representatives noted that both membership and income fluctuates much more in response to international than national events. Staff members offered this assessment on the basis of the success of various appeals for contributions, as well as from member comments and letters: "International hunger events have made the major difference to Bread's membership, much more so than anything done domestically in the last ten years."[37]

Consequently, the organization remains extremely sensitive to fluctuations in the preferences of a small group of supporting members. In the interest of organizational survival, the group has developed an adaptive ability to shift its political agendas in order to align with member preferences.[38] Its consistent reliance on private contributions and steadily increasing income totals indicate that private-sector resources expanded over the decade and point to the tactical utility of subtly redefining agenda priorities during a period of political turmoil.

The second private group, CBPP, was founded during the first Reagan term explicitly in response to the redirection in budget priorities championed by the New Right. The group was organized with the support of contributions from private foundations, benefiting particularly from a major grant from the Field Foundation. From its 1981 founding, the group counted on private sources for more than 90 percent of its income and generated the remaining 10 percent from the sale of publications and from conference revenue. Through the first Reagan term, total group income grew by 60 percent annually, for a total increase of 334 percent. Rapid growth continued through the second Reagan term, increasing by an additional 112 percent. As table 3 indicates, CBPP experienced a tremendous expansion in available resources between 1981 and 1985, almost entirely because of contributions from private sources.

Over the decade, CBPP also became more self-sufficient, generating a growing share of its income in-house. Reductions in the percent of total income from private contributions (down 4.3 percent) resulted largely from an increasing share of revenue raised through programs and publications, which accounted for 7 percent of total income by 1985.

The CDF also strongly expanded during the 1980s. While its rate of growth lagged behind the CBPP, CDF began the decade with one of the largest endowments of any citizens groups in Washington. It was certainly the strongest member of the hunger lobby. Through the decade, CDF relied on a combination of public contributions, program revenue, and dividends from an extensive stock portfolio. In contrast with the organizational turmoil confronting many antipoverty groups during the first Reagan term, total CDF income continued to rise—by more than 37 percent by 1985 and by an additional 42 percent over the second Reagan term. Today, the group counts on more than $12 million in annual income and holds a comparable endowment in reserve.

Resources, including income, provide the fodder for political activity. During the 1980s this meant privately funded groups were in better position to address the political concerns of the social-welfare sector. This relation also highlights the inherent contradiction in public-interest group representation of the poor: Political crisis may promote group mobilization, but the shrinking budgets that all too often accompany political crisis for this interest sector undermine that same potential to mobilize.

POVERTY ADVOCACY GROUP ALLOCATION DECISIONS

What effect did the markedly different budget situations of these groups have on their strategic actions? We can begin to answer this question by looking at group allocation decisions. Patterns of allocations comment on organizational decision making in light of political goals and financial constraints. Expenditures reported in annual reports, financial statements, and IRS 990 forms may be divided into two broad categories of group spending: political activities (including a wide variety of governmental and grass-roots actions, issue analysis, and lobbying) and organizational maintenance (including staff and office costs). The IRS scrutinizes the actions of tax-exempt organizations to ensure they do not devote a substantial share of their activities to lobbying.[39] Consequently, much of their policy work takes the form of issue analysis.

The importance of resources for political action suggests that changes in group budgets and levels of political activity will be directly related. An overview of the spending patterns of these six groups supports this contention. The three privately funded groups responded to budget expansion by increasing their political action. Conversely, the three federally

Table 4. Annual Expenditures and Percent of Total Devoted to Political
Activity, 1981–1988

	CSWPL	FRAC	CNI	BFW	CBPP	CDF
1981 spending ($)*	765,574	817,628	1,354,227	1,234,455	164,617	1,709,719
1985 spending ($)*	784,253	615,208	230,691	1,681,709	593,467	2,864,493
1988 spending ($)*	603,917	751,066	271,808	1,902,323	1,294,663	4,329,937
Percentage change in total spending:						
1981–1985	+2.4	−24.8	−83.0	+26.6	+360.5	+67.0
1985–1988	−29.9	+22.1	+17.8	+13.1	+118.1	+51.2
Change in percentage of total devoted to political action: 1981–1985†	−8.0	+30.2	−17.9	−8.3	+18.0	−2.6
1985–1988†	−2.7	−4.7	+2.0	+0.8	+1.2	−0.6

*All figures are given in constant 1980 dollars.
†Figure includes issue analysis and lobbying.
Sources: IRS 990 forms, audited financial statements, and annual reports.

funded groups each had to reduce their programmatic spending. An overview of the shifting spending patterns of these groups is presented in table
4, which documents annual expenditures and the percentage of the total
devoted to political activity and to management by the six groups in the
sample.

For the CSWPL, total expenditures rose 2.4 percent by 1985 despite an 18
percent funding loss. This slight increase reflects deficit spending by the
group (e.g., by more than 10 percent in 1985), a trend that bodes ill for the
group's long-term survival. Through this period, issue analysis and lobbying remained the two largest group expenses, accounting for at least 65
percent of total annual spending. Total spending on these areas of political
activity, however, actually fell by 8 percent from the 1981 high of $632,919.
This decrease inversely reflected demand for the center's services over
these same years. The long-term effects of budget cuts are seen even more
dramatically during the second Reagan term, when total spending by
CSWPL fell by nearly 30 percent and spending on political action fell by an
additional 2.7 percent. In other words, less money was available to spend,
and a shrinking percentage of what remained was spent on political action.

One effect of this cutback is seen in the annual level of congressional testimony delivered by the group. While CSWPL continued to invest in political
activity, it shifted efforts away from Washington DC, leading to reduced
levels of congressional testimony. Averaging two appearances per year

during the Carter presidency, CSWPL appeared before Congress approximately once every other year between 1982 and 1987.[40] This reduction suggests that, despite a stated commitment to national involvement, CSWPL was forced to reduce its national advocacy presence.

The FRAC also lost income between 1981 and 1985, accounting for a 25 percent reduction in total spending, as well as a $50,000 deficit in 1985. Between 1985 and 1988, total spending rose by 22 percent. Unlike CSWPL, however, FRAC actually increased by 30 percent its income devoted to lobbying and issue analysis in the face of budget cuts by severely reducing management costs (down 36 percent) and by virtue of the infusion of new sources of income. It also raised money by subleasing office space. This income proved to be a mixed blessing: It provided needed funding but also committed FRAC to a reduction in facilities and resources (also seen in 50 percent staff reductions in 1981 and 1982). During the second Reagan term, proportionate spending on political action declined somewhat, as the group successfully reestablished a more secure organizational footing.

According to representatives, the decision to leverage FRAC to pay for congressional lobbying and public information campaigns was critical to the group's survival.[41] Two of FRAC's efforts during this period were exposing the administration's plan to list ketchup and pickle relish as vegetables in the school-lunch program and providing technical support to the CBS television documentary *People Like Us*, which portrayed a family sliding into homelessness.[42] The highlighted changes in the school-lunch program seemed to confirm the advocates' charge that the White House was heartless.

In 1980 the combination of lobbying and issue analysis accounted for 64.6 percent of FRAC's expenditures, roughly the equivalent of CSWPL. As a percentage of total income, however, FRAC's spending on political activity increased markedly from 1982 on, rising to 67.5 percent in 1982 and to 85.7 percent in 1984. In short, while both total income and total spending fell, the proportion of spending on political action actually rose. Shifting increasing shares of a diminished budget to political action might well have undercut a fragile organizational existence. In this case, however, the group's strategic decision to spend on political action not only meant short-term political viability but also led to maintained visibility and, consequently, an ability to attract new supporters.

Some indication of this resilience is seen in levels of hearing participation. During the Carter years, FRAC averaged 5.2 appearances annually. During the first Reagan term (and despite income cuts and organizational retrenchment), FRAC actually maintained its presence in congressional hearings (appearing 5.5 times annually).

A different set of opportunities and strategic options were available to the CNI, which suffered much more severe budget reductions than any of the other groups in the sample. Scrambling to survive, CNI cut general spending, disbanding its training division and refocusing its efforts into its newsletter, *Nutrition Weekly*, to report on food programs and budget proposals.[43] As table 4 indicates, total group spending on political activity and management fell by some 83 percent by the end of the first Reagan term. This cut heavily affected organizational operating funds and all but eliminated funding for political action. Spending on management and infrastructure was reduced by 75 percent. In 1985, spending on political action was pruned to an eighth of 1981 levels and rose only marginally by 1988. The magnitude of income loss meant a total reduced investment in political action of more than 80 percent.

The CNI lost most of its institutional base, scaled back its size and activities to operate on reduced revenue and, in the process, was virtually forced out of national political action. With the loss of income, CNI shifted to a more traditional relation with funders, offering a selective incentive in return for membership dues. More than 80 percent of CNI income in 1984, for example, came from subscribers.

In 1981, spending on political activity was double that allotted to organizational maintenance. By 1984 spending on management consumed more income than political action. Further evidence of reduced political activity is seen in CNI's pattern of testifying before Congress. Between 1976 and 1981, CNI was one of the most active participants in the hearing process, appearing a total of forty-nine times (an average of 8.2 appearances yearly). This is the highest incidence of hearing participation among groups in this study. Over the six years after the 1981 budget cuts (between 1982 and 1987), however, CNI appeared before Congress only fourteen times (averaging 2.3 visits per year), a reduction of more than 70 percent.

One critical factor in the relation between budget cuts and political action is the magnitude of the cuts. Groups such as CSWPL that undergo marginal losses may have to weigh the advantages of turning against existing funders versus retrenching to ride out political firestorms. Groups suffering devastating losses, such as CNI, may be too injured to recover and may not have the option of limping along on a reduced stipend. Does this relation between the magnitude of changes in income and possibilities for political action hold for groups with expanding incomes as well? If so, we would expect group activity to increase in response to the combination of expanding demand and resources.

Table 4 presents the allocation patterns of the three privately funded groups in the sample as well. The first of these groups, BFW, increased spending by 26.6 percent between 1981 and 1985 and an additional 13 percent by 1988. During the first Reagan term, the group's budget grew by more than 25 percent, and absolute spending on both political activity and management rose as well. As a percent of total spending, however, political action actually decreased by 8.3 percent by 1985 and remained roughly constant through 1988, in part reflecting the general expansion in the group's budget.

While BFW's budget situation alone does not explain the decreased emphasis on domestic political action, group representatives suggest that Third World famine was the primary concern of members through the early 1980s.[44] The group responded in turn by devoting more attention to overseas activity during the 1980s. Second, unlike FRAC, BFW leaders believed their organization was best served by seeking only incremental changes during a period of intense presidential and congressional concern with budget shortcomings. It appeased members and avoided congressional and administration animosity by concentrating on Third World hunger. In this way, BFW sought to ride out the storm of intense political controversy.

The decision to shift organizational priorities followed from what one representative described as a long-term advocacy strategy during the 1980s.[45] This strategy was premised on the belief that seeking incremental changes would prove more effective than confrontational tactics. By avoiding direct confrontation, "Bread sustains its reputation as both serious and moderate." This combination, one representative suggested, can be quite difficult for an ecumenical organization like BFW to maintain, since it is expected to stress morality while keeping a blind eye to the realities of political bargaining.[46] "There is a belief [in Congress] in the accuracy and credibility of what we do, more so than for other ecumenical organizations. By taking the long-term view of policy making we are adding capital to our credibility."[47] Maintaining a long-term view, a representative explained, allowed BFW to work with elected officials more interested in the budget than in poverty while more vigorously addressing member concerns with hunger abroad: "Legislators are more amenable to organizations which do not attack members worried first and foremost about budget considerations."[48]

The group's pattern of involvement in congressional hearings also indicates this programmatic shift. Its total level of testimony increased on domestic issues (up from 1.8 appearances a year during the Carter administration to 3.2 appearances a year during the first Reagan term). In comparison, BFW's rate of testimony on international poverty and hunger tripled over the same period.[49]

In contrast, CBPP pursued a very different strategy of political engagement with the Reagan administration, not only spending more on domestic political activity but also devoting more time to hearings on domestic social welfare. The organization's total spending doubled between 1981 and 1982 and rose by an additional 68 percent by 1985, for a five-year growth of more than 360 percent. Over the next three years, CBPP continued to grow, with total spending doubling once again by 1988. In total, CBPP spending increased nearly fivefold over the two Reagan terms. The group initially devoted 61.6 percent of total spending to political activity. This percentage rose until 1985, when the group devoted nearly 80 percent of total outlays to political activity. After 1985, spending on political activity rose by an additional percentage point. In the context of a rapidly expanding budget, this 18 percent supplement represented a fourfold increase in absolute terms. Over this same period, spending on organizational maintenance decreased as a percentage of total outlays, from 35 to 15 percent. This reduction indicates the rapid growth in the group's total income.

Financial expansion also translated into increasing testimony levels for CBPP. From its 1981 founding, it quickly established its access to congressional hearings, appearing more than six times yearly by 1985.

Group representatives suggest a number of factors contributed to the growth and niche building of CBPP, including the recognized expertise of its founder, Robert Greenstein, generous initial support from the Marshall Field Foundation, and several strategic decisions. Able to avoid federal grants, CBPP sidestepped the funding cuts experienced by some groups. Consequently, CBPP defined itself in opposition to the White House. Further, it focused on providing ongoing analysis of administration budget proposals. Targeting the White House's attempts to set welfare agendas, CBPP provided competing budget analyses that reached Congress and the interest-group community at the same time as OMB budget projections. In so doing, CBPP divested the administration of some of its rhetorical advantage.[50]

The sixth case study, the CDF, also responded to increased income with political mobilization. The group's budget and output both grew over the decade. As table 4 indicates, CDF total spending between 1981 and 1985 increased by 67 percent and grew by an additional 50 percent before the end of the Reagan years. As with the other private groups, absolute spending on political action increased, accounting for a slight decline of nearly three percentage points in total outlays devoted to political action between 1981 and 1988.

In congressional hearings as well, CDF again solidified its leadership position among antipoverty advocates. During the Carter presidency, CDF averaged 7.3 appearances a year. Over the Reagan years, by contrast, its annual average increased to 12.5 appearances.

RESOURCE MOBILIZATION AND SURVIVAL TACTICS

The six public-interest groups considered in this chapter maintained varying levels of political presence on the national scene over the 1980s as a result of both resource constraints and strategic choices. All three federally funded groups faced funding cuts during the first Reagan term. Each responded with tactical choices reflecting this income loss, yet the divergence in their actions mirrors their varying perceptions of organizational and political realities. Meanwhile, the three privately funded groups benefited from expanded resources that figured heavily into their tactical responses as well.

The CSWPL reacted to reduced income by curbing their national political activity and working to diversify their support base. Increased fundraising follows from budget cuts as groups scramble to offset lost federal revenues. As we would expect, CSWPL doubled its spending on fund-raising, from 3.0 to 5.9 percent of total outlays. In this way, diversification of support helped the organization survive the funding crisis. Yet even with private contributions, the group ran a deficit in three of the six years examined and reduced spending on issue analysis and lobbying in both absolute and relative terms.

By contrast, FRAC lost a higher percent of income, was forced to raise funds aggressively, and consequently maintained its levels of political output. Survival meant lean years, staff reductions, budget deficits, and salary cuts. Restructured budgets from 1982 on drew heavily from a mix of individual, corporate, and foundation grants. Notably, group respondents suggested that political activity in and of itself also proved a successful fund-raiser, since the group became identified with vigorous opposition to the Reagan administration's social-welfare policies.[51] This identification allowed FRAC to carve a new policy niche, establishing an issue domain distinct from the federal government from which to attract concerned funders. Some of FRAC's more visible activities through this period included exposing the Reagan administration's attempt to classify ketchup and relish as vegetables in the federal school-lunch program and consulting on the CBS documentary *People Like Us*.[52]

Despite losing patronage and income, FRAC maintained its political presence in the nation's capital. In comparison with CSWPL's decision to stay within the (increasingly constrained) parameters afforded federal grant recipients, FRAC's decision may have been reached out of desperation. While CSWPL lost 40 percent of its federal funding, FRAC's federal income fell by more than 65 percent. In this respect, its access to federal money was nearly sealed off, forcing it to find new means to survive. From a position of greater desperation, the group's strategic decisions resulted both in maintained advocacy and in subsequent financial recovery.

The situation of the CNI allows for further extending our interpretation of the relation between organizational threats and political action. In fact, the group's response suggests this relation is curvilinear. In contrast to CSWPL, which chose to work within the bounds of reduced income, and FRAC, which responded to more substantial loss by redefining its organizational mission and strategic action, CNI lost more than 80 percent of total income and cut spending on both organizational maintenance and political action accordingly. This comparison suggests that, while a degree of resource contraction will increase the attraction of strategic maneuvering, severe resource withdrawal preempts strategic action and induces wholesale retrenchment if not collapse.

By contrast, privately funded groups were spared the organizational constraints imposed on their federally funded counterparts. Nevertheless, a parallel exists between the two categories of organization in that all six groups chose tactics that reflected their self-perceptions.

Primarily reliant on member contributions over and above dues, BFW defined its policy environment in response to internal pressures. During the 1980s, contributors were concerned with international relief efforts, and the group's political output reflected this preference. Graphic coverage of the plight of famine victims far outweighed media attention to domestic poverty during the first Reagan term.[53] As a result, while BFW's resources expanded and political output increased, its focus shifted away from domestic hunger.

This shift indicates one problem with private funding. Public and private foundation concern can be extremely variable, causing groups, of necessity, to shift their political energies and underlying value systems to maintain access to resources. This finding expands our understanding of the relation between group action and membership commitment. As we would predict, potential members are attracted to particular organizations because of the political activity these groups pursue.[54] The evidence from these antipoverty groups suggests that groups can also be tremendously sensitive to member preferences and are willing to shift their political agendas to reflect shifts in the value systems of their members. Bread For the World, for example, pursued a programmatic agenda that clearly responded to shifting member preferences.

For the CBPP, the Reagan challenge actually created the possibility for organizational growth and political action. The group defined its agenda from scratch so that its mission and actions took shape in opposition to Reagan-era federal social-welfare initiatives. Should the political pendulum once again swing toward increased commitment to welfare provision, this self-definition would need to be amended. Group literature from early in the Clinton administration reflects this shift. CBPP encouraged supporters to rally behind President Clinton's budget, for example, and to oppose congressional balanced-budget proposals.[55] Both the budget and political activity of CBPP expanded in response to rapidly growing private resources. The same is true for the CDF, which roughly tripled its budget and kept pace with an expanding lobbying agenda. Both cases lend support to the pluralist expectation that groups will mobilize in response to heightened issue salience.[56] More accurately, their success should be viewed in the context of tremendous budget fluctuations in this issue sector, indicating the importance of establishing access to funders, governmental institutions, and policy domains for continued group action.

These six cases indicate the complex ways that resources contribute to public-interest group maintenance and strategic action. All six groups chose organizational and political tactics in light of their own understandings of what was needed to preserve their organizations and engage in political action—yet their positions and perceptions led them in very different directions.

Seven tactical initiatives have been identified among these six groups, indicating the ways that groups formulate their actions and identities to reflect changing values and opportunity structures. Table 5 presents a number of the principal tactical choices made by these groups. All six groups devoted growing portions of their output to fund-raising. Services were offered to attract and hold members. New political issues and tactics also allowed several groups to redefine their operating space so as to avoid administration antagonism. For some of these groups, new tactics have meant more confrontation. For other groups, new tactics meant trying to survive the Reagan years without further antagonizing funders.

The actions taken by these six groups suggest that, as with social-movement organizations, attacks on the resources of public-interest groups will cause them either to curtail their activities or pursue increasingly confron-

Table 5. Principal Tactical Choices of Antipoverty Advocacy Groups

Tactical Choices	Funding Situation of Groups Adopting This Strategy	Organizational Ramifications
Grantmanship	All groups (both stable and unstable)	Divert resources to fund-raising
Increasing member services	Unstable	Divert resources to member services
Providing direct services	Unstable	Divert resources to relief services
Establishing new issue domains	Secure	Reframe policy agenda to group's advantage
Adopting new political tactics	Both types (both stable and unstable)	Evaluate and potentially sever existing alliances
Organizing new groups	Secure	Capture resource streams and establish new groups
Retrenchment	Unstable	Curtail or cease political activity

tational tactics.[57] Shrinking resources drove CSWPL from political confrontation. As the same window of opportunity all but closed for FRAC, the group was pushed outside of institutional channels and was consequently forced to redefine itself and its relation to the government. As this same window slammed shut on CNI, the group retrenched and concentrated its few remaining resources on producing its newsletter.

At the same time, groups with expanding access to resources will annex political domains and work to secure access to funders. For example, BFW shifted toward international issues in pursuit of member approval. Similarly, during the 1980s, the CBPP defined its mission and agenda on the premise that the federal government's War on Poverty coalition could reconvene around a private group oriented against a clearly defined antagonist in the White House. This orientation had already begun to shift in the early Clinton years. Organizational theorists describe subtle shifts in organizational values in terms of an "organizational matrix," delimiting both the value criteria and, by extension, the participants in a sector of interest-group activity.[58] Manipulating the values, missions, goals, and tactics that characterize a field of interest activity allows groups to cope with uncertainty in their resource fields, uncertainty that all groups wish to minimize.[59]

These cases give substance to our understanding of the relation among resources, public-interest-group survival, and political action, demonstrating that budget realities define attractive market positions and tactical choices for advocacy groups independent of the political challenges they face. While these six groups all prioritized political action during the Reagan years, in practice their responses were quite different and reflected not simply absolute incomes but also specific facets of their budgets and—more important—each group's own perceptions of its organizational security.

5

Politics by Other Means: Poor People's Protests in the 1980s

Squeezed out of institutional access by an antagonistic presidential administration and skittish funders, advocacy groups for the poor were thrown into turmoil. Some groups weathered this period successfully, but others were not so fortunate. When resources are scarce, groups are forced to scramble for their own survival. Under these circumstances, political activity may be given second priority. In the process, an already-marginalized constituency may be left without its principle political voice.

However, as with other marginalized groups, institutional advocacy is only one form of political action available to the poor. A second possible response to constrained institutional access is increased protest in the form of direct action, civil disobedience, street protest, and riots. These forms of activism are available to even the most marginalized groups and, under the right conditions, can tremendously influence political decision making. Direct action gives voice to challenging groups while defying basic norms of political interaction. Protest can also signal that widespread concerns have not been addressed by mainstream policy-making. The emergence of protest may signal the rise of mass-based social movements.

According to Doug McAdam, the emergence of noninstitutionalized tactics conveys a rejection of established, or "proper," channels of conflict resolution and will raise concern among elites for the threat they pose.[1] With respect to tactics, McAdam tells us, "It was their fundamental powerlessness *within* institutionalized channels that led insurgents to abandon 'proper channels' in the first place. Accordingly, insurgents must chart a course that avoids crippling repression on the one hand and tactical impotence on the other. Staking out this optimal middle ground is exceedingly difficult. Yet failure to do so almost always spells the demise of the movement."[2]

One of the principal leaders of the homeless movement that emerged during the 1980s offered a similar assessment of strategic and tactical choices: "We were interested in equalizing the dialogue. Other people have the power of voting . . . of political campaigns. The poor, however, aren't consumers. They don't do the things that matter in capitalist society and therefore are ignored. This is where we come into the picture. We scare the crap out of people: putting our lives and freedom and health on the table in order to equalize the dialogue."[3]

While national poverty fighters were squeezed out of institutional channels, outsider groups increasingly gained agenda space by taking to the streets in protest on behalf of the poor and homeless. Their actions reframed the politics of poverty in terms of an emerging homeless movement. Over the 1980s, both new and existing antihomelessness groups adopted an increasingly vocal and confrontational political posture. Some of the most vocal groups to emerge included the National Union for the Homeless (NUH), the Community for Creative Non-Violence (CCNV), and the Association of Community Organizations for Reform Now (ACORN). The tactics of these various advocacy and social-movement organizations reflect the disparate strategies that have characterized many American movements, ranging from congressional lobbying to street protest.[4]

Protesters, and the social movements which encompass them, use means beyond those accepted by mainstream society, including such nonconventional political behavior as boycotts, street theater, rioting, gatherings, demonstrations, and civil disobedience.[5] Historically, protest politics has been critical to the struggles of weak challenging groups, including the poor, racial minorities, and the homeless. Protest tactics, when effectively employed, *amplify* the voice of small groups and call attention to the resonance between small groups of protesters and larger, more powerful constituencies. Dramatic events command the attention of the media and the public at large. Apprehensions about possible rioting and protests following the civil-lawsuit trial in the Rodney King case in April 1993, for example, were stoked by the riots of the previous spring after the initial police-brutality trial. Anticipating a second season of rioting in 1993, the Los Angeles City Council empowered Mayor Tom Bradley with emergency "riot prevention" powers. Las Vegas soon followed, granting Mayor Jan Jones authority to impose curfews and to curtail sales of liquor and firearms. Local media in both cities stepped up the number of public-service announcements playing on the themes of "togetherness" and "community" and broadcast the toll-free number of a "facts hotline" to defuse rumors and panic about rioting and violence.

Dramatic instances of collective action may be the most fundamental way to heighten awareness of the existence of the poor in American society. As Piven and Cloward put it, "Whatever influence lower-class groups occasionally exert in American politics . . . results from . . . mass protest and the disruptive consequences of protest."[6] For groups without other resources, protest may provide the last line of political defense. Homeless activists, for example, seized and occupied HUD-repossessed houses in eight U.S. cities on 1 May 1990. Their actions drew attention to federal foot-dragging on the pledge to turn 10 percent of these homes over to the homeless.[7]

Collective protest occurs as individuals come to recognize their common identity in pursuit of some cause and against a shared antagonist. For a protest movement to arise from the traumas and grievances of daily life, "people have to perceive the deprivation and disorganization they experience as both wrong, and subject to redress."[8] In the process of collective action, disparate individuals forge a common identity, square off against their adversaries, and demand political redress. In so doing, protesters both respond to and work beyond institutional politics. Protesters "not only band together to act on their interests but also act in ways that directly, visibly, and significantly affect other people's realization of their interests."[9]

Protest politics occupies an uneasy position in American democratic theory. Through the 1950s and 1960s, most research concluded that protest threatened the workings of healthy democracies. Accepted political participation, in contrast, made use of standard, institutional channels of access. Legitimate political groups would gain political voice commensurate with their persuasiveness and size. These characteristics would ultimately lead to political action, electoral power, and policy success. Protest politics, therefore, broke the rules of democracy by challenging the sanctity of standard procedures and institutions of participation. Protest was thus aberrant behavior, indicating some kind of breakdown in the norms of democratic society, some pervasive psychological angst or anomie, society's failure to provide effective "intermediary associations," or the collective feeling of "relative deprivation" experienced by some group.[10]

The role of protest politics in democracies was widely reevaluated in the 1960s, as many traditionally silent groups chose street protest over interest-group or electoral activity. The waves of student protest, antiwar demonstrations, and the civil-rights movements led analysts increasingly to characterize protest as a rational political choice made by individuals unlikely to win political concessions through more conventional approaches.[11] In this light, protest is a logical political response by marginalized groups.

Strong, compelling reasons must be present for protest to develop. Protesting is a high-cost strategy, demanding intense personal commitment and running the risk of repression and misrepresentation. Repressive states with little tolerance for protest will crush it. Relatively open regimes that permit easy access to decision making defuse potential protest by offering other means of access and concessions.

Social movements, including the civil-rights movement, the women's movement, the environmental movement, and the antinuclear movements, have played an important role in contemporary American politics. All these efforts have involved demonstrations, protests, and demands for political change. They have also all succeeded in attracting the support of widespread groups of Americans as well as that of political elites and media personalities. Americans have grown accustomed to a half-million protesters converging on Washington DC in support of issues ranging from gay rights to abortion reforms. Still, moments at which widespread collective action is likely to occur are limited in occurrence and in duration.

ORGANIZING TO MOBILIZE: STRATEGIC THINKING AND TACTICAL CHOICE

Within the political context defined by public policy, White House rhetoric, levels of issue salience, and media attention, activists maneuver to increase the attention directed at their cause in order to galvanize support for their actions and, most important, to pursue desired concessions. Activists' tactics place them somewhere between mainstream political action and radicalism. In choosing actions, organizers must adopt tactics that appear legitimate to mainstream society without alienating the majority of the movement they seek to represent. Tactics must be politically acceptable and viable, must clearly demonstrate the plight of the movement, must attract sympathetic groups within the public, and yet must be seen as more than simply rituals. Effective tactics must actually challenge authority and provoke a response.

Successful instances of collective action will balance several demands: resonating with the public, drawing attention to movement concerns, and challenging the authority of institutional actors. As a result, a successful tactical repertoire is both structured and interpretive.[12] The language and actions of earlier successful movements are incorporated as they elicit intended responses, and actions are tailored to make them appropriate to the realities of a given situation. According to Thomas Rochon, "The ideal [tactical choice] is . . . convincing with respect to political authorities, legitimate with respect to potential supporters, rewarding with respect to those already active in the movement, and novel in the eyes of the mass media."[13]

It is seldom easy or immediately accepted when challenging groups rise up against the perceived "natural" order of business and social structures. For movements to gain adherents and supporters, they must successfully claim to represent a legitimate political position. Legitimacy can be sought by appealing to cultural forms and symbols. In the civil-rights, labor, and anti-nuclear movements, for example, church parishes and leaders provided leadership and organizational resources, and the forms of religious worship were incorporated into the styles, language, and actions of these movements.[14] "Prayer meetings, like public rallies, are characterized by their mass nature and have as their purpose the articulation of issues of justice and the public evidence of community, political, and religious solidarity. Religious symbolism, hymns, sermons, and mass prayers are typical of protest rallies even as these meetings are distinguishable from more typical religious services by their explicit political rhetoric and appeals for justice."[15]

Conducting prayer meetings and using religious symbols and symbolic action (e.g., ritualistic fasting) may invest protesters with religious legitimacy and further their claims to higher authority.

In challenging more powerful actors in society, protesters may be met by violent repression. During the workers movements of the early twentieth century, for example, "goon squads" would try to intimidate labor leaders and break the collective spirit of workers.[16] Repression can also be routinized through legislation. With the adoption of the Taft-Hartley Act in 1947, the possibilities of collectivization among industrial workers were heavily circumscribed by law, by rigid structures of industrial relations, and by union acquiescence.[17]

We can identify five aspects of direct political action critical to interest representation: types and targets of action, numbers of participants, involved organizations and supporters, the degree to which protesters' objectives are widely understood and embraced, and government responses. These facets of protest politics suggest five issues to consider in evaluating the direct-action events undertaken by protesters for social justice in the 1980s.

First, what actions did activists undertake? Tactical choices available to protesters make up a "repertoire" of available action that must be used carefully to sway political authorities, attract potential supporters, reward active participants, and capture the imagination of the mass media.[18] As with effective tactics, well-chosen targets of protest lead to more media and, subsequently, national attention. Actions leveled against the White

House and the president, for example, are better suited to media coverage than coordinated actions targeting multiple offices of Congress. Although policy may be enacted in Congress, the moral weight of the Reagan reforms clearly rested on the White House.

Second, how many people participated? The competing claims of legitimacy in pluralist systems leave little "political space" for extrainstitutional dissent. Large or widely discussed protests can overcome this handicap by establishing graphically the support generated by protesters' policy claims. In general, mass mobilization is a fundamental goal of protest organizers. At the same time, small groups are able to perform guerrilla-type actions not available to their large, unruly counterparts. Many of the acts committed by radical environmental groups such as EarthFirst!, for example, could only be undertaken by and succeed for small groups.

Third, what groups were involved? As chapter three indicated, antipoverty organizations may provide the infrastructure for mobilization. Certain organizations have established clearer access routes to the media and to institutional political actors. The CDF, for example, is widely recognized for having national expertise on the problems confronting poor children. Neither congressional hearings nor rallies for poor children can afford to exclude CDF and retain their political legitimacy. Elite supporters may also lend expertise or celebrity to collective-action events. Martin Sheen's personal involvement in homeless protests with the CCNV drew media mention, for example, adding to the newsworthiness of events in which he appeared.

Fourth, what were the objectives of the action? Clearly defined objectives, symbolically linked with the tactics chosen by protesters, demonstrate the legitimacy of activists' demands, reaffirm their commitment to the cause, broaden a movement's support base, attract outside resources, and potentially lead to policy concessions. Where objectives remain vague, the energy of protest is unlikely to translate into political gains.

Finally, what did government do in response? Positive response, whether symbolic or tangible, may dissipate protest while opening channels for mediated, institutional access. Conversely, repression, particularly through arrest, can either authenticate the actions of protesters while painting authorities as heavy-handed or greatly slow the mobilization of dissent and make potential actors wary of getting involved.[19]

FRAGMENTS OF A MOVEMENT: HOMELESS PROTESTS IN THE 1980S
Over the 1980s, a series of protests broke out in the United States over issues of poverty and homelessness. The dominant strain of actions were

undertaken in support of the homeless.[20] In fact, as the decade progressed, nearly every account of poor people's protests in the United States explicitly mentioned the plight of the homeless. There are a number of reasons for this concentration. First, homelessness became a particularly graphic problem, dramatically thrusting the poor into public consciousness in a way that chronic poverty alone fails to do. Second, homelessness is a problem that reached its present magnitude only during the 1980s. In this sense, homelessness appeared as a fairly new problem, unburdened by the historical baggage that other facets of social justice carried and sidestepped the stigma of longstanding federal welfare programs in terms of the rhetoric of poverty relief and ambiguously supported programs. As a result, homelessness is a more likely candidate for widespread issue recognition and concern. Greater numbers of people living on the street asking for handouts make homelessness a fact of life for many nonpoor people and provide dramatic evidence of a growing public problem. In this way, homelessness provided a new and newsworthy edge to the recurring problem of poverty in America. In the words of a homeless advocate, "The attention span of Americans is so short that keeping homelessness on the agenda so long was our central task and our principal success."[21]

These facets of homelessness offset the difficulty of measuring its prevalence and, consequently, its seriousness as a social and political problem. Estimates of the number of homeless Americans in 1984 ranged from a quarter of a million by HUD to three million by the CCNV. A decade later, studies suggest there are seven hundred thousand people homeless on any given night. Half of these people regularly live on the street. Meanwhile, between seven and 12 million Americans have been homeless for some period over the last five years.[22] In 1987, the U.S. Conference of Mayors reported a 25 percent increase in demand for social services by the homeless in 22 major American cities and noted that the fastest-growing segment of the homeless population was families with young children.[23]

Between 1 January 1980 and 31 December 1989, there were fifty-nine protests specifically conducted by advocates for and among the homeless in the United States that gained coverage in the national press.[24] Between 1 January 1990 and the summer of 1992, an additional fifteen homeless protests achieved this level of recognition. Beyond these recorded actions, the plight of the poor and homeless was invoked in more than two hundred protests for other causes. For example, protesters angered by the MX missile decried the federal government's skewed priorities while millions of Americans remained poor. Protesters of U.S. support of the Nicaraguan

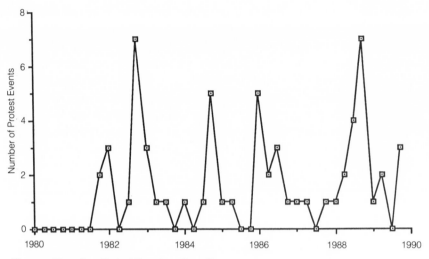

Figure 1: Homeless Protest Events, 1980–1989
Source: Nexis OmniFile (New York Times, Washington Post, etc.), 1980–1989.

contras, for example, suggested that poor and homeless Americans were more appropriate targets of aid and support. In part, these protests against militarism invoked homelessness in order to tie other concerns to the burgeoning attention devoted to a growing homeless population.[25]

Figure 1 presents the distribution of homeless protests over the 1980s, showing a pronounced cycling of protest events between 1982 and 1990. As this figure indicates, protest events occurred with greatest frequency during congressional election seasons (i.e., 1982, 1984, 1986, and 1988). In fact, nearly 70 percent of homeless protest events were undertaken in congressional election years (forty of the fifty-eight events). The strong link between the congressional election cycle and homeless protests suggests that advocates recognize the advantages of launching actions during this period.

Election years expand political opportunities for challenging movements first through the heightened uncertain prospects of elected officials as they face reelection. Second, electoral seasons bring increased media attention to national political rhetoric on issues including poverty. Electoral seasons are also when legislative agendas are established for the upcoming political session. In this regard, operating space, established by legislative work and electoral cycles, can be turned to the advantage of protesters. We explore this relation further in the next chapter.

The amount of attention Congress devotes to an issue such as domestic poverty is, in turn, a powerful factor in determining the level of media attention devoted to the same issue as well as the ways in which poverty will be interpreted and "framed" by the media.[26] As Laura Woliver has put it, "In a society where majority rules, an issue has to be constructed in a way acceptable to the majority."[27] Consequently, as media attention is attuned to political rhetoric during election seasons, protesters tune their actions accordingly to force poverty onto policy agendas.

Returning to figure 1, we see an absence of events before the fall of 1981, despite much earlier indications of the Reagan agenda. Reasons for this lag include lower levels of homelessness in the 1970s and greater advocate access to a relatively sympathetic administration before the OBRA cuts and full Reagan transition.[28]

A TACTICAL REPERTOIRE FOR HOMELESS PROTESTS

Protests by organizations championing the rights of the poor and homeless drew from a particularly rich and varied tactical repertoire. Organizers must choose targets symbolically connected to their cause in order to legitimate their actions. At the same time, targets must be linked to desired concessions. Where to focus their efforts can be particularly troublesome for the poor and homeless, who have no readily identifiable antagonist and who depend on the combined efforts of city, county, state, and national governments, as well as on the philanthropy of private relief organizations, churches and charities.

In their protests, advocates for the homeless imported traditional movement activities such as marches, demonstrations, and rallies and innovated actions that drew attention to the particular plight of poor and homeless people in an otherwise-affluent society. Two themes emerge repeatedly in their innovations: the crushing misery of life without permanent shelter and the links between mounting homelessness and government inaction.

Reflecting the difficulties of life without shelter, activists and the poor raised tent cities and shantytowns and served free meals at the base of the national monuments in Washington DC. Similarly, activists singled out the White House, which provided a powerful symbol of unequal housing opportunities and the complicity of the president. Homeless protests fanned out across the country, as protesters across the country occupied deserted and condemned buildings, claiming them for the homeless. Taking over federally owned buildings, protesters argued they were simply prodding HUD to fulfill its pledge to devote more resources to the homeless.

The activists of Homes Not Jails, an Oakland, California, group, typify

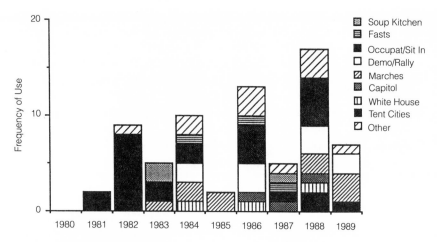

Figure 2: Protest Tactics, 1980–1989
Source: Nexis OmniFile (New York Times, Washington Post, etc.), 1980–1989.

the goals and actions of these activist-advocates. Representatives of the organization identify three goals underlying their actions. They conduct covert squats in abandoned buildings, moving in homeless people under cover of darkness in order to secure them temporary shelter. They also conduct public takeovers of abandoned houses as an act of civil disobedience, attracting media, community, and government response. Finally, they lobby city government directly and participate in writing guidelines for treatment of the homeless.[29]

Perhaps the urgency of homelessness and the intense concern it invoked was demonstrated most graphically as protesters undertook a series of well-publicized hunger fasts. Figure 2 summarizes the types and distributions of actions undertaken by homeless protesters over the 1980s. Over these years, the principal target of nationally reported protest actions was the federal government, and specifically the president. Some of the most popular and most often repeated tactics of the 1980s focused on the Reagan administration. In total, twenty-one events incorporated actions which targeted President Reagan directly.

Early in the decade, protesters constructed tent-city "Reaganvilles" and "Reagan Ranches," reminiscent of Depression-era Hoovervilles. These encampments were prototypical movement actions in two ways, pinning blame for homelessness on the president and linking protest action and emergency relief efforts. This link continues to characterize homeless protests today. In 1993 and 1994, for example, the city of San Diego contemplated constructing a temporary tent city to house the homeless. Ironically, protesters raised just such a tent city to protest both a lack of affordable housing and city rousting policies.

At the October 1982 opening of Pittsburgh's twenty-tent Reagan Ranch, ACORN organizers called attention to the similarities between 1980s homelessness and the Great Depression. In both eras, they noted, people lined up for hours for donated meals.[30] To celebrate the opening of a twenty-five-tent Reagan Ranch in New Orleans in 1982, protesters held a "Nancy Reagan Fashion Show for the Depression Minded."[31]

These tent cities rose across the country over the 1980s and ranged in size from one or two tents in Washington DC to more than thirty-five tents and cardboard shacks in Atlanta. The shelters seem to have captured the attention of the media because of their meagerness. Reporters noted the shantytowns comprised "frayed tents, dirty blankets, cellophane and cardboard."[32]

During his presidency, President Reagan looked out over twelve successive iterations of the Reaganville tent city in Lafayette Park, despite a city ban on permanent shelters in the park and periodic police roustings. Washington DC's ban on permanent shelters, in turn, was challenged by the ACLU, which argued that the freedom of speech of the homeless was in jeopardy. The ACLU argued that people without property have few ways to express themselves politically other than by putting themselves in harm's way. At the White House's urging, the city continued to dismantle the tent cities in Lafayette Park, generating more media attention for the protesters, who simply rebuilt the shelters.[33]

Reporters nationwide repeatedly mentioned the connections between encampments of temporary shelters and the general plight of the homeless. Reports concentrated on the number of homeless occupying the tents, the severity of weather conditions during the occupation, and the adequacy of meals provided. Journalistic accounts keyed into the "authenticity" of the tent cities. Stories that questioned the legitimacy of protests focused on the nature of the occupation. Were the tents occupied and the occupants really homeless? A report on one Houston tent city suggested there were no actual homeless people among the protesters.[34] Another account questioned whether most shelters were occupied and whether they reflected the actual prevalence of homelessness versus the political agenda of a small core of hardened activists. Responding to these charges, activists argued that their numbers were small because the homeless were reluctant to participate even in protests from which they would directly benefit because their involvement would mean giving up their claims to relatively safe shelters such as highway underpasses and sidewalk steam grates.

The Reaganville camps not only graphically portrayed the plight of the homeless; they also juxtaposed the poor with the rich and powerful, well symbolized by the grandeur of the White House. Protesters focused on the White House as emblematic both of the Reagan administration's "mean spiritedness" and the dichotomy of American opportunity. As a target of action, the White House offered another advantage to the movement. Whereas Capital police policies are relatively tolerant of many kinds of peaceful marches and demonstrations, the codes of conduct concerning the White House have always been more strict, calling for immediate response. Pausing on the White House driveway or attempting to pass through the gates or climb the fence is grounds for immediate arrest.[35]

For all these reasons, the White House has long been a popular target for protesters. Activists know their actions will be closely scrutinized, both by authorities and the media. Also, as collective actions aimed at the White House will elicit quick and certain response, the combination of protest action and police reprisal may heighten the newsworthiness of a particular action. Eleven actions (nearly 20 percent of the total) were launched against the White House. During the course of a monthlong "call to civil disobedience" against the White House and Congress in October 1984, protesters hung the president in effigy in Lafayette Park, declared the White House a homeless shelter, laid sleeping mats across the drive and walkways, chained themselves to the White House fence, and released cockroaches on the White House tour. In still other actions, protesters led marches to the White House, prayed within its gates, splashed blood against the gates and fence, climbed the fence, and blocked traffic on Pennsylvania Avenue.[36]

In the same way, President Reagan's ranch near Santa Barbara, California, also became a target of homeless protests. In the mid-1980s, the growing homeless population in Santa Barbara was terrorized by vigilante attacks after a series of conflicts between the affluent community and the homeless. In an effort to curb the numbers of homeless people, city police invoked a seldom-observed public sleeping ban. The homeless had also been thwarted in their attempts to register to vote because they lacked permanent addresses. In response to their exclusion from voting rights and what they viewed as a police preference for ousting rather than protecting them, a group of homeless people marched the twenty-eight miles from Santa Barbara to the Reagan ranch.[37] Two years later, more than one thousand homeless people were assembled to re-create the march to the Reagan ranch, this time under the direction of CCNV advocate Mitch Snyder. Calling Santa Barbara the "Selma of the Homeless Movement," Snyder pressed the city to curb its persecution of the homeless, rescind the ban on overnight public sleeping, extend voting rights, and strengthen police protection to the homeless.[38]

Timed to coincide with President Reagan's vacation at the ranch, the planned march attracted the attention of reporters from around the country. Santa Barbara consequently agreed to rescind its ban on public sleeping and to encourage voter registration among the homeless. In turn, the march was canceled.[39] Both the 1984 march and the aborted 1986 march demonstrated that pockets of poverty remained even in the most affluent parts of the country and again implicated the Reagan administration in the plight of the poor.

Some of the most dramatic actions aimed at the president were the hunger strikes undertaken by CCNV members led by Snyder and Carol Fennelly. The symbolic connection between hunger and fasting is not lost to protesters. The Hunger Project, for example, conducts an annual one-day fast. César Chavez launched a five hundred–day "chain" fast, in which advocates, political leaders, and celebrities each went without eating for one day in recognition of the poverty of farm workers. More recently, members of the House of Representatives joined Democratic Representative Tony Hall of Ohio in fasting in protest of the cut in funding to the Select Committee on Hunger's appropriation. The profound personal sacrifice endured during a long-term fast shaped much of the coverage that protesters received over the decade.

Mitch Snyder gained a reputation for being the leader of the homeless movement by embarking on at least five hunger strikes in the 1980s, each specifically indicting Ronald Reagan for worsening hunger and homelessness in America. Each fast also appeared to result in direct and substantive concessions from the federal government. Snyder and CCNV first announced a fast for the homeless during CCNV's first major protest outside Washington. From a tent encampment in downtown Kansas City, twenty members of CCNV embarked on the fast to call attention to the disturbing irony of the government's store housing of surplus food (in Kansas City and elsewhere) while millions of Americans went hungry.[40] After the group fasted for thirty days, Secretary of Agriculture John Block announced the administration would "give more government owned food to the poor." Victorious, CCNV returned to Washington to "continue their day-to-day jobs of helping the homeless find shelter and working in soup kitchens."[41]

The most dramatic and widely reported hunger fast lasted through the fall and winter of 1984, when Snyder went fifty-one days on water alone. Members of CCNV began an open-ended fast on 15 September, pledging to starve until the Reagan administration changed its social-welfare policies.[42] Over the next two months, the group engaged in a number of public protests, including the month-long "call to civil disobedience" against the White House preceding the 1984 elections.[43] During the fast, Snyder lived outdoors in CCNV's Lafayette Park tent city, facing the White House. Finally, at the direct order of the president, the administration agreed to fund renovations of a massive Washington DC homeless shelter, which has since grown to more than 1,400 beds.[44] Snyder ended his fast at this "change of heart and policy on the part of the Reagan Administration," but not before losing more than sixty pounds.[45]

Winning funding for the shelter proved to be a mixed blessing for CCNV. They gained critical support and a politically important concession but simultaneously were consequently forced to demonstrate their ability to run a massive shelter. According to a CCNV representative: "We changed the minute we opened those doors [to the shelter]. Where we had been a small, Christian community, now we had to run a massive organization. . . . Opening the shelter in [19]84 plucked out the center of the community. . . . Running this whole organization destroyed our community."[46]

Homeless activists also took aim at Congress. As figure 2 indicates, actions targeting the Capitol building and Congress occurred with greatest frequency during congressional election years (particularly in 1984, 1986, and 1988). Unlike those aimed at the White House, however, actions directed at Congress run the risk of fragmentation. In confronting Congress, protesters had to balance their potential to have an impact on specific pieces of legislation with broader goals including calling public attention to their plight and expanding their support base. Still, Congress was the site of a number of important collective actions over the decade. In August 1982, protesters erected a "Congressional Village" tent city in conjunction with the Reaganville encampment in Lafayette Park.[47] The following year, in a larger coordinated assault, about three hundred people held a sit-in on the Capitol grounds and blocked Capitol Hill traffic in the "People's State of the Union" protest.[48]

The year 1986 was marked by the massive Hands Across America event. Designed to raise funds and consciousness for the issues of poverty and homelessness, Hands Across America attracted the participation of some five million people, including media celebrities and politicians, and drew major corporate sponsorship. Even President and Mrs. Reagan eventually joined this event, which was effectively a protest against poverty in America. The Reagans joined hands with children as the nation-crossing chain was routed across the White House lawn. Funds raised by Hands Across America were distributed to hunger and homeless organizations. Participants also received information about local service agencies and advocacy organizations.[49] This event marked a turning point in actions over the decade. After Hands Across America, protest events were generally larger, targeted directly at specific pieces of legislation, and tactically more conventional.

Later in the decade, protesters again found cause to single out Congress for actions. Calling for passage of proposed homeless-assistance legislation, in 1987 the CCNV set up a soup kitchen on the Capitol steps to dramatize under the gaze of Congress itself the number of people who relied on emergency relief.[50] Protesters undertook another massive "Call to Civil Disobedience" during the 1988 electoral season. Again led by the CCNV, advocates undertook a month-long campaign against the Capitol and against individual members of Congress. With CCNV stewardship, groups came from around the country to Washington DC to call attention to the nation-wide lack of affordable housing.[51] Over the month, activists held sit-ins and demonstrations and coordinated an almost daily series of arrests.[52] These serial actions, according to CCNV representatives, were critical to "keeping the pressure on Congress to act. . . . Arrests six days a week kept the issue in the news."[53] Many of the actions took the form of sit-ins in congressional offices. Nine homeless advocates from Tucson, Arizona, for example, held a sit-in in the office of Republican Representative Jim Kolbe of Arizona for nine hours after they were unable to persuade the congressman to support increased aid to the homeless. The protesters were arrested when they refused to leave at the end of the day.[54]

Two weeks later, one hundred protesters from Cleveland gathered in the Capitol rotunda to sing protest songs and were quickly arrested. Other demonstrators attempted to "evict" Senator Jesse Helms of North Carolina from his office.[55] A week later, forty-five protesters from midwestern states filled the office of Republican vice-presidential nominee Dan Quayle of Indiana, asking for increased federal aid to public housing.[56] Ten days later, activists from Columbus, Ohio, held a sit-in in the office of Representative John R. Kasich of Ohio and vowed not to leave until he "promised to support a $25 billion annual increase in housing aid."[57] Wearing cardboard placards with the names of homeless people who had died in the streets of Columbus, group members vowed to "disrupt business as usual" because, they said, "business as usual is killing people."[58] Finally, on the eve of the November elections, demonstrators took over Senator John Heinz's Washington and Philadelphia offices and called on the senator to stop his "support of Ronald Reagan's policy of building up the military at the cost of domestic spending."[59]

The month-long civil disobedience produced daily assaults on Congress. After Democratic gains in the 1986 elections, 1987 appeared to hold the promise of further policy gains for supporters of progressive domestic initiatives, with major action taken to expand social welfare through Massachusetts Representative Barney Frank's Affordable Housing Act and the subsequent McKinney Homeless Assistance Act. The 1987 vote on the McKinney Act followed the "Grate American Sleep-Out," in which a dozen members of Congress joined a small crowd of movie stars and activists in a sleep-in on steam grates to demonstrate their solidarity with the homeless.[60] As figure 1 suggested, the combination of an electoral shift and heightened public and legislative attention resulted in one of the largest surges in protest activity surrounding homelessness in 1988 and in the arrest of more than 230 demonstrators.[61]

With the transition from the Reagan to the Bush presidencies, the tenor of homeless protest changed noticeably, responding to the shifting political opportunities of the new presidential administration's promise of a "kinder and gentler" America, coupled with the specific provisions of the McKinney Act, which had gained legislative agenda space and provided a vehicle for lobbying efforts. Collective-action events began to snowball in size and at the same time began to target much more specific goals. Protests later in the decade were directed at proposed legislation, as compared with the earlier general condemnations of the Reagan agenda. In this way, the appearance of an opening for policy concessions led to heightened challenger mobilization and political activity while, *at the same time*, leading to more specific and constrained advocacy agendas.

The major protests through 1988 and 1989 drew crowds much larger than earlier actions, and protesters gravitated toward more mainstream and accepted tactics, as opposed to earlier guerrilla actions in which small bands of protesters stirred up trouble and were quickly arrested. By April 1988, *The Nation* declared the homeless movement in full swing.[62]

Figure 3 documents the size of homeless protests over the 1980s and indicates the distribution of the sizes of events across the decade. As figure 3 indicates, there were more large protests later in the decade and size became less of an issue in determining whether protests would be reported.

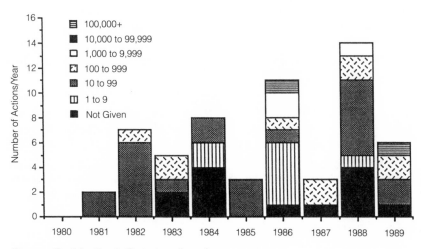

Figure 3: Participation in Protests, 1980–1989
Source: Nexis OmniFile (New York Times, Washington Post, etc.), 1980–1989.

While we can offer a number of factors that help to explain the distribution of events across this period, including the proximity of congressional elections and legislative agendas, participation rates are more difficult to characterize. More than half of the total events reported in major American news outlets drew fewer than one hundred participants during the 1980s. In fact, all but one of the actions before 1983 were of this size. Fewer than 25 percent of these events were reported to have drawn the support of more than one hundred people. Overall, approximately 8 percent of homeless protests during the 1980s had more than one thousand participants, and only two protests of this 8 percent drew crowds larger than one hundred thousand. Contrary to the expectation that the number of protesters involved in an action is critical to the level of coverage it receives, more than 22 percent of event reports fail to indicate how many people were involved.

Through 1982, all but one event had fewer than one hundred participants. The one exception was a rally and demonstration at a Columbus, Ohio, tent city and soup kitchen in October 1982, which drew five hundred participants.[63] By 1986, the size of protests grew more diverse, with one action drawing several hundred participants, and two actions attracting more than one thousand. Between 1987 and 1989 the size of protest events ranged from the very small to gatherings of more than 100,000 supporters. Typical of the larger events held later in the decade was an election-eve rally in November 1988. Approximately two thousand people joined in a march and rally in Washington DC to call attention to the "crisis of home-lessness." Led by CCNV, the rally featured celebrities including Dr. Benjamin Spock and Cher and culminated with a massive sit-down, blocking Capitol Hill traffic and leading to the arrests of 377 people, including the eighty-five-year-old Spock.[64]

Even larger crowds gathered the following April in both Washington DC and San Francisco to protest Bush administration cuts in social programs. Leaders of the marches charged the Bush administration with attempting to eliminate social programs while adding to an already-bloated defense budget.[65] Meanwhile, in Washington DC about two thousand people marched from the Capitol to the White House in pouring rain, again to protest Bush administration policies. Harkening to earlier actions, these protesters raised a tent city on the Capitol grounds and called for more federal assistance to the homeless.[66]

In October 1989, several hundred people in San Francisco and some two hundred thousand in Washington marched on behalf of the homeless. Protesters converged on Washington from around the country to participate in a three-day protest seeking increased federal funding for low-income housing. Activists led small groups of homeless people and social-service representatives on lobbying missions to congressional offices and government agencies, hammering home the point that low-income workers were "only a paycheck away from disaster."[67] Protesters also met with Housing Secretary Jack Kemp, who pledged to clean up the scandal-plagued Department of Housing and Urban Development and to make 10 percent of HUD's inventory of foreclosed single-family houses available to the homeless in 1990. Foot-dragging on this pledge would precipitate the takeovers of abandoned HUD homes the following May in eight U.S. cities by homeless advocates.[68] The 1989 March on Washington was billed as the largest homeless protest "since the federal government, under Reagan, began cutting back on housing assistance."[69]

CHOOSING CONTENTION: THE TWO FACES OF COLLECTIVE ACTION

Collective action is not undertaken in a vacuum. Rather, it is a response to the tangible constraints imposed on people's lives. This is to say that there is a strongly *interactive* component to protest politics. Collective action is only likely to emerge in response to specific and tangible challenges, and the tactics adopted by social-movement participants are responses to specific challenges to their lives. In this sense, tactics reflect the need for specific responses appropriate to individual situations. As a result, collective action is similar across contexts, as protesters attempt to gain concessions from a position of relative weakness. Individual protests, however, are distinct in that they reflect the specific context in which they emerge.

One important facet of the interactive nature of collective action is the type of response from economic and government authorities it precipitates. Vigorously suppressed mobilizations are presumably extinguished or driven underground. Conversely, mobilizations welcomed into institutional and party politics are dissipated and diffused by mainstream political actors. The type of state response to collective action, therefore, is important not only for shaping and framing insurgent demands but also for determining the likelihood of gaining concessions. Evidence from the civil-rights movement suggests that repressive responses to protest may heighten levels of national attention and may ultimately lead to policy concessions.[70]

How important was repression of homeless protesters both for gaining issue attention and subsequent concessions? The principal means of curtailing protest in the United States is by arresting or harassing protesters. For many potential participants, even the threat of arrest is enough to dissuade them from action.[71] Most of the respondents in one recent study of activism in the 1980s conceded they were ultimately unwilling to go to jail for extended periods of time for their beliefs.[72]

The threat of arrest and the negative sanctions that face "troublemakers" can be powerful deterrents to conscience constituents.[73] Repression, however, may backfire on authorities by strengthening the legitimacy of a challenging group, affirming the bond between participants, attesting to their "authenticity," and setting them collectively apart from authority figures.[74] Arrests become a badge of movement participation and provide graphic footage for television crews. In fact, arrests often gain more attention than the kinds of causes that led protesters into the streets.[75] In this way, arrests galvanize protesters, legitimate their actions, and inform the public about movement demands.[76]

Figure 4 presents the distribution of homeless protest events over the decade in terms of the number of arrests that occurred. This figure suggests that the presence of arrests need not be as central to media coverage as is often suggested. In fact, coverage of most protests (65 percent of the total) reported few if any arrests. As a determinant of a protest event gaining coverage, therefore, the tactical utility of arrest is suspect. In 16 percent of the events, between one and nine protesters were arrested, while in another 16 percent, arrests reached double digits. Twice over the decade,

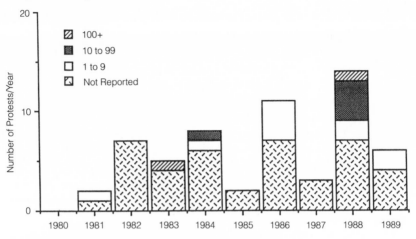

Figure 4: Arrests Reported in Homeless Protests, 1980–1989
Source: *Nexis OmniFile (New York Times, Washington Post, etc.), 1980–1989.*

more than one hundred people were arrested in such actions. In the "People's State of the Union" protest on the lawn of the Capitol in January 1983, 162 people were arrested for blocking traffic until "Congress declares a national state of emergency concerning homelessness."[77] Capping the 1988 election season civil-disobedience campaign, 333 arrests were made among the two thousand marchers calling for a stronger (i.e., fully funded) McKinney Homeless Assistance Act.[78]

THE ROLE OF ORGANIZATIONS IN PROTEST

We have touched on the ambiguous relation between organizations and protest. Yet an organizational infrastructure can be critical to coalescence and action.[79] The short-lived successes of the welfare-rights movement, for example, came through mobilization and disruption but might have been extended had there been leaders "not of the mobilization-disruption genre," as Jacqueline Pope has stated. "Their absence impeded the movement's natural progression to its next stage."[80]

Perhaps the most important resource available to the homeless was the organizational potential manifest in several key advocacy groups. Organizing the homeless, however, is a difficult task. According to Brad Kessler, "It is difficult to cut through the suspicion and cynicism found on the streets and also the endemic problems of drugs, alcohol, depression and mental illness. Homeless people generally do not congregate in one place, and when they do, it is in shelters and welfare hotels, where organizers of

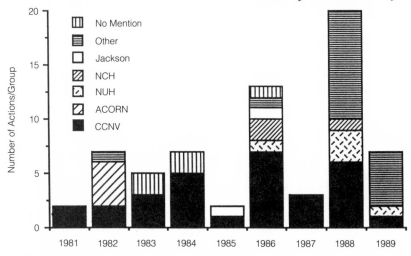

Figure 5: Organizations Active in Protest, 1981–1989
Source: Nexis OmniFile (New York Times, Washington Post, etc.), 1981–1989.

any kind are not welcome . . . [creating] a climate of terror and uncertainty."[81]

The relation between mobilization and political organizations remains controversial. Some observers argue that only through effective organizing can the energy of social movements be harnessed into a lasting force for social change.[82] Others remain dubious of the role organizations play in expressing and channeling poor people's demands. Frances Fox Piven and Richard A. Cloward argue that most of the organizations thrown together in the course of a poor people's movement fade away quickly. "As for the few organizations which survive, it is because they become more useful to those who control the resources on which they depend than to the lower class groups which [they] claim to represent."[83]

Over the 1980s, the vast majority of reported collective-action events by the poor and homeless were launched under the banner of one of a small number of political organizations. These included ACORN, NUH, the National Coalition Against Homelessness (NCAH), and CCNV. While the NUH claimed to be the only advocacy group empowered by the poor and homeless themselves, each of these organizations stresses its organic relation with the homeless community.

Figure 5 characterizes homeless protests in terms of the groups in the forefront of the actions. As figure 5 indicates, ACORN, CCNV, and NUH spearheaded most of the actions recorded. Other groups that appeared included the National Coalition of the Homeless (NCH) and organizations working with the Reverend Jesse Jackson. Figure 5 indicates both the importance of existing, well-established groups early in the decade and the proliferation of new organizations later in this period.

Early in the decade, tent cities were erected across the country under the leadership of the CCNV and ACORN. Through the middle of the decade, via hunger strikes and the 1984 "call for civil disobedience," CCNV was consistently at the forefront of homeless actions.

Either by itself or in combination with other groups, CCNV led twenty-eight actions over the decade. It also spearheaded the major tactical innovations of the homeless movement, including the Reaganville tent cities, publicly situated soup kitchens, White House actions, calls to civil disobedience, and hunger strikes. In turn, the media increasingly associated CCNV with the voice of poor Americans. Nowhere is this more evident than in a United Press International report of a seven hundred–person counter-inaugural march led by Jackson protesting Reaganomics and homelessness. The reporter covering the event was careful to note CCNV's *absence* and to indicate that the group planned no events for the day.[84]

The group's hunger strikes may have gone far toward identifying it with the homeless movement as well as capturing more attention for the homeless movement than any other actions. Subsequent articles on CCNV and Mitch Snyder consistently mentioned the fifty-one-day fast. Snyder's life was dramatized in a television movie starring Martin Sheen, who subsequently accompanied Snyder on a number of protest actions. For the remainder of the decade, and indeed until his death, Snyder's position as spokesman for the homeless remained secure in the media. Perhaps most significant, the media identified Snyder as the person able to elicit the direct and personal intervention of President Reagan.[85]

But even CCNV was pulled in two directions by its self-conception. The group functioned, and continues to function, as an activist organization while running a set of homeless shelters with nearly fifteen hundred beds. After the federal government finally made good on its promise to renovate CCNV's main shelter, the group was put in the position of fulfilling its pledge to run the massive shelter. Devoting increasing time and energy to running the shelter diverted the group's energy from direct action. Their political efforts were further splintered by Snyder's death in 1990.

The small group of organizations in figure 5 is mentioned repeatedly in coverage of both national and local protests and quickly came to be identified as the leadership of the homeless movement. Like their institutional counterparts, these groups worked to reconcile an inherent tension between middle-class leaders and an impoverished constituency. Organizations such as the Coalition for the Homeless historically were white, middle class, and professional while serving a poor, marginally employed, and disproportionately minority population.

Advocacy and activist organizations believed the empowerment of poor communities was fundamental to their mission. For antipoverty groups like FRAC and CSWPL, this commitment meant constructing organization and decision-making structures drawing from poor communities. Activist groups went to greater lengths. The NUH claimed twenty thousand homeless members by 1988.[86] Exactly what this figure means is unclear, given the tentative links between the NUH and its membership. Nevertheless, advocates from many groups expressed their concern with the potential for increasing distance from their constituents and cause. Representatives for homeless organizations repeatedly stressed their homeless membership. Advocacy group representatives consistently suggested poor people's membership was essential to their organization. For the CCNV, internal decision-making processes were designed to empower all members. To escape the trappings of formal organization, CCNV paid no wages to its members and made no distinction between leaders and members, and CCNV members wore the same clothing, ate the same food, and lived in the same shelter as the people they served. But even these types of efforts were at times circumvented. The media, for example, looks for particular faces to identify as leaders. For CCNV, this meant that Mitch Snyder and Carol Fennelly were consistently singled out as the leaders and representatives of the organization.

As existing organizations gained increasing attention in the press and concern with homelessness grew, the number of organizations participating in protest events expanded as well. By 1988, half of the events reported mentioned groups other than the principal five (ACORN, CCNV, NUH, NCH, and that led by Jackson). Between March 1993 and March 1994, nineteen groups leading homeless protests were mentioned in the national press.[87] Several of the principal groups from the 1980s remain active, including CCNV and ACORN. In addition, there are a number of groups too new or small to be listed in the 1993 IRS guide to tax-exempt organizations. Like Homes Not Jails, most of these organizations are locally based and concerned with a particular city's homelessness policies.

THE LESSONS OF PROTEST

Through their protests, poor people and activist organizations illustrated the urgency and hardships of poverty, provided focal points for organization efforts and media attention, periodically attracted large crowds and celebrity and legislative interest, and gained at least grudging legislative concessions in both homeless-assistance legislation and related social-services funding. The homeless movement borrowed tactics and symbols from earlier, successful movements, including the civil-rights campaigns, and borrowed cultural and religious symbols in its struggle for recognition and legitimation.

These protest events provided a forum for translating the condition and concerns of the homeless to a broader audience or, rather, to several specific audiences including policymakers and the media. Protests generally included graphic, symbolic actions—splashing blood on the White House gates, unrolling mats across the White House drive and declaring it a homeless shelter, turning bags of cockroaches loose on the White House tour to remind onlookers of the conditions under which many poor Americans lived, or even jumping into a giant cherry pie baked by the Young Republicans. All these events gained notice for their novelty and the image they created. Through these dramatic actions, hunger and poverty were pushed toward public-policy agendas.

Besides demanding political response, protests provided the homeless with an organizing tool. From tent cities to soup lines, many of these actions transformed service provision into political action. The various tent cities across the country claimed to provide shelter or warm meals or winter clothes to people forced onto the streets. Organizers attracted the poor through these services and simultaneously created protest events. Providing traditional relief services in unusual locations and incorporating charity into protests also created powerful images of need, hopelessness, and despair. Tent cities in front of the White House and soup lines snaking around the Capitol underlined the immediacy and pervasiveness of poverty against the grand backdrop of Washington monuments. In these examples, providing relief became part of a political campaign rather than a diversion from it.

Over the decade, collective actions in Washington and nationwide attracted the participation of hundreds and even thousands of protesters and attention from the media. To trace the policy impact of these actions, it is necessary to consider the context in which they arose and on which they made an impact. Antipoverty advocacy and activism are contextualized in terms of public concern and government attentiveness. The evidence of homeless advocacy and activism allows us to address two questions: First, what effect does political context have on the likelihood that marginalized challengers will be able to mount a political action in the United States, and what form will their political action take? Second, in what ways does the political action of the marginalized offer a means to shape policy agendas?

6

Political Opportunity and
Antipoverty Activism

Poor people and their supporters attempted to influence the policy-making process in the United States in the 1980s both directly through social-movement mobilization and indirectly through interest-group activity. Their demands, however, were often muted and inconsistent, and we are left to wonder what impact they had on the direction of domestic welfare policy. Despite advocates' efforts, the Reagan reforms had a clear and lasting impact on subsequent welfare spending. Again in the early 1990s, federal retrenchments have led to cuts in social services in many parts of the United States while individual states prune their contributions to federal programs such as Medicaid. That cutting aid to the least advantaged is an acceptable response to budget constraints is perhaps the most telling and lasting legacy of the Reagan revolution.

This chapter presents a discussion of the relation between political action in support of social welfare and the larger policy-making process. There are two facets to this relation: the ways in which the political process, and particular "political opportunity structures," channeled and shaped antipoverty advocacy and the effect of these tentative advocacy efforts on policy-making.

Confronted by economic recession, shrinking social services, cuts in federal support, and ever-decreasing health care, advocates for the poor in the 1980s attempted to mobilize and push for political accommodation. Yet these representatives generated little consistent political response, either through widespread interest-group or social-movement activity. Not only do the resources necessary for political action remain difficult for the poor to generate, but the allies that had come to their support at other times were absent. Unions, cities, and civil-rights groups were caught up in their own battles with the White House, encroaching regulations, and dwindling memberships.

Still, for supporters of popular participation in politics, flashes of political response were generated, against long odds, by the poor and their allies. Protesters took to the streets in guerrilla actions, mass demonstrations, and protests across the country. Meanwhile, private giving rose, new antipoverty groups formed, and advocates won passage of the McKinney Homeless Assistance Act.

Efforts to combat the domestic agenda of the Reagan and Bush administrations ranged from street protest to congressional lobbying and indicated that at certain times even the most marginalized groups will engage in collective action. Political change can throw a sector of issue advocates into turmoil. The strong electoral position of the Reagan coalition early in the decade constrained the opportunity for maintaining and expanding social services in this country because members of Congress were reluctant to side with advocates, seemingly against the wishes of the voters. Coupled with a mounting deficit, a budget-driven policy-making process emerged. Administration insiders conceded they tolerated large deficits *in order to* squeeze the political Left out of decision making.[1] Confronted with large deficits, government-sponsored liberal think tanks would lose funding and be silenced. In short, allowing the deficit decreased the political space available for supporters of social justice. The White House carefully used the prominence and attention focused on the president to orchestrate a rhetorical attack on the "failed policies of the past" that Reagan believed characterized the legacy of welfare since the New Deal. The combination of a cowed Congress, a rhetorically strong president pressing for a particular vision of social policy, and a budget that seemed to demand increasing fiscal austerity bounded discussions of poverty policy early in the decade.

As avenues of access traditionally available to advocates of the poor shrank, issue representatives were forced outside traditional channels of access. The number of homeless protests recorded in the national press rose from zero in 1980 to a handful in 1981 and then to more than ten in 1982. As avenues for institutional access are withdrawn, representatives will seek other venues through which to press their grievances. In this case, the quest took them into abandoned buildings and the Capitol rotunda. In short, attacks on social-justice programs, coupled with withdrawn means of institutional access, *constrained* institutional action as well as *heightened* levels of noninstitutional participation by the poor and their supporters.

No lasting poor people's movement has emerged, however, to mobilize a national network of conscience constituents, capture media attention, and demand political action. No broader wave of mobilization took up issues of social justice. In this sense, the call for action that underlay the civil-rights and antiwar efforts of earlier eras failed to reconfigure around the poor and politically marginalized in the 1980s. Instead, issues of poverty and homelessness have become submerged under the rising strains of activism on behalf of a national health-care agenda, AIDS, environmental justice, and children's welfare.

What outcomes followed the fragmented mobilization of the 1980s? Was the usually weak voice of the poor amplified by their actions? While little activity was generated, were actions well chosen and carefully placed? Did this political activity ultimately elicit desired responses?

A POLITICAL-PROCESS EXPLANATION OF POOR PEOPLE'S MOBILIZATIONS

The political-process model suggests that patterns of interest mobilization follow from the flow of resources and the specific political opportunity structures that channel and delimit opportunities for mobilization.[2] Political opportunity structures fix the level of openness of political systems to challengers and their demands. Extremely tolerant ruling coalitions will co-opt and assimilate dissent while extremely repressive regimes will crush challengers and their agendas.

At certain times, policy upheaval sparks independent, noninstitutional mobilization in the form of academic and journalistic attention, for example, as well as isolated instances of activism—which in turn attract media attention and heighten public concern. Increasingly salient issues attract resources including mass memberships, elite support, and foundation grants. Responding to expanding resources, new groups form and existing groups mobilize. At the peak of a cycle of mobilization, masses of citizens may take to the street in protest, policy experts, celebrities, and government elites will publicly "defect" to the challenging movement, existing advocacy groups experience a surge of membership, and new groups form.[3]

In electoral democracies, governmental response to widespread public sentiment can be sure and swift. Democratic regimes are eager to extend symbolic overtures to popular challengers, taking up their issues in presidential rhetoric, for example, or scheduling congressional hearings. There are dangers, however, facing advocates trying to navigate beyond symbolic concessions. Gaining agenda space in the committee hearing process, for example, may co-opt and diffuse groups' energies, alienating groups from more strident factions in their own movements and dissipating support from conscience constituents, who believe government is responsive to their concerns.

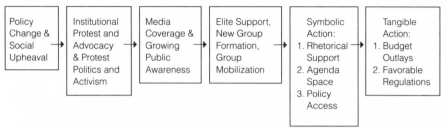

Figure 6: The Mobilization Model

Sometimes insurgents successfully maneuver beyond symbolic politics and gain tangible concessions, which can include budget appropriations and favorable regulations. At other times, governments respond by suppressing challengers and withdrawing institutional access for groups and individuals deemed too radical.[4]

The 1980s were a period of shifting political opportunity for poverty advocates. The Reagan administration closed institutional channels to activists and advocates. The resulting shakeup within the advocacy community simultaneously led to the emergence of new voices in the policy process and quelled the activity of long-standing advocates.

Figure 6 links a number of the critical steps in insurgent mobilization, simplified as a linear process whereby a gradual building of awareness and concern with an issue leads to increased mobilization and an increased likelihood of political response. These steps are critical to generating a movement, although they are by no means exhaustive. To generate widespread mobilization, issues must sear into collective consciousness and appear to be public-policy issues, that is, posing a crisis to society.[5] Emerging issue positions are represented by communities of experts and policymakers who define issue positions, frame agendas, and indicate appropriate courses of action.[6]

Elected officials, in turn, respond to swings in national mood and mobilized constituents by working to bring new constituent demands under institutional consideration.[7] When policy crisis, expert advocacy, and public attention converge, policy windows open, issues are covered extensively in the press, academics and experts press the urgency of the emerging issue, the public begins to mobilize in support of the new concern, and advocates for the issue thus gain support and attention.[8] In a sense, during periods in which policy windows open, advocates find themselves propelled into action through a process of mobilization beyond their control. Conversely, during periods in which policy windows are closed, advocates find that all their energy and ingenuity is unable to gain them agenda space. Certain policy windows open predictably while others appear unexpectedly. Policy entrepreneurs push preferred solutions through these windows of opportunity.

At certain times, crises lead to the recognition of social problems. The impetus for recognition may come from expert and media attention or from protest actions or riots. A good example of this process was seen in the "discovery" of poverty in America in the early 1960s. President Kennedy's declaration of a war on poverty owed much to both the civil-rights movement and to Michael Harrington's *The Other America*. Multiple currents of unrest in American society urged the president to action. The struggles of the civil-rights movement graphically depicted economic and political injustice (and provided a forum for challenging the policies of the Eisenhower administration). Harrington's attack on American complacency and the affluent society gave a causal dimension to the problem and suggested both reasons behind and possible responses to the cycle of poverty.[9] Reading Harrington (or Dwight MacDonald's review of Harrington in the *New Yorker*) predisposed Kennedy to perceive responses to poverty in Harrington's terms. Harrington's attention to structural causes of poverty and universalistic programs shaped the War on Poverty well into the Johnson presidency.

For issues to generate dramatic collective action, they must capture the public's imagination. The media is critical to this process. Media attention expands the audience for an issue, allocates agenda space to it, frames potential solutions, and identifies relevant actors, including both champions and antagonists.[10] Charles Kuralt's 1960 documentary for cbs News, *Hunger in America*, followed the path of the Field Foundation's Physician's Task Force as it sought out pockets of chronic, persistent, and life-threatening hunger within an otherwise-affluent society. Through this documentary coverage, the intractability of misery among America's poor gained attention in living rooms across the country. Piven and Cloward stress this same idea in terms of the importance of a "rising curve of antipoverty rhetoric" that must be present in order to make a moment ripe for widespread concern with poverty.[11]

As issues gain recognition, relevant advocates are identified, antagonists are targeted, and resources are mobilized. Increased issue attention leads to growth in mass memberships, philanthropic, corporate and government funding, support of experts, celebrity advocacy, and increased access to government (making possible either concessions or co-optation).[12] Collecting these resources is also critical so that advocates can voice their concerns most effectively. The Marshal Field Foundation's Physician's

Task Force sought out pockets of poverty in the 1960s, generating media and congressional attention. After holding hearings on hunger in America, Congress approved funding to construct the Office of Economic Opportunity in 1964. During the 1950s and 1960s the Ford Foundation also advanced a strong social-justice agenda that not only emphasized expanded availability of relief services but also actively sought to nurture the political and social life of poor communities.[13] This same process of patronage was at work in the preparation and publication of Charles Murray's *Losing Ground*, which contributed to the conservative attack on the theory and practice of American welfare in the 1980s.[14] Murray received production and research support from the conservative Manhattan Institute, which also undertook responsibility for marketing the book.

Resources for political advocacy can also follow from increasing concern with a particular issue among the public at large. Millions of Americans linked arms in the Hands Across America event in 1986.[15] While Hands Across America failed to advance a particular political agenda, it was an important part of the story because it demonstrated a massive and nationwide concern with hunger and poverty. In this respect, the event marked a turning point in the 1980s in terms of the size and type of antipoverty protests that subsequently occurred, as well as levels of media attention and institutional response directed toward poverty.

SOCIAL IMPACT: THE "NEW POOR" AND AMERICAN POLITICS

In part, the degree to which an issue rallies public support follows from its presentation and framing. Issues that attract widespread concern must be seen as recent, public, and urgent. Importantly, these issues must also be amenable to human action.[16] While little concerted national mobilization met the Reagan reforms, there was cause to believe such a mobilization might emerge, given the academic and journalistic accounts of a "new poverty" that was certainly recent, urgent, and amenable to human action. While poverty rates fell steadily over the 1960s and held relatively level through the 1970s, the first major increases in American poverty since the Kennedy years occurred during the first Reagan term. We see this increase in both the number of Americans in poverty and in the percentage of the country below the poverty line.

Figure 7 presents the number and percent of Americans living on incomes below the official poverty line since the late 1950s. While poverty rapidly declined through the 1960s and held steady through the 1970s, it began to rise in 1979 and continued to climb through the first Reagan term.

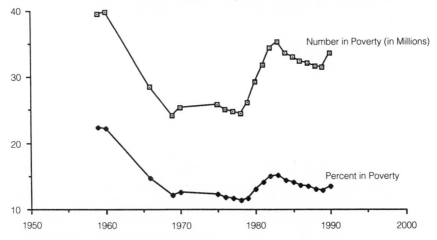

Figure 7: Number and Percent of Americans below the Poverty Line, 1959–1990
Source: Statistical Abstracts of the United States: 1992.

Against a steady series of budget cuts in low-income programs, the poverty rate climbed rapidly from 1980 to 1983 and then increased more gradually through 1985. By the winter of 1985, 15.3 percent of the country (almost thirty-five million people) were officially poor, up from less than 12 percent in 1979.

SEEDS OF PUBLIC AWARENESS: ACADEMIC AND JOURNALISTIC INTEREST

Poverty generates intense interest at particular times in American history and then fades from national consciousness for long periods. Robert Salisbury has noted the irony in American political representation, in which "specific political movements tend to rise and fall within relative brief spans of time, but many of what might be called movement streams, including peace, civil rights, and moral reforms . . . , are quite enduring parts of the political system."[17]

The worsening condition of poor Americans gradually entered national consciousness through media coverage, which was concentrated on the human-interest side of rising poverty rates and the changing demographics of poverty, particularly the growing numbers of children and whole families in poverty. According to the House Committee on Ways and Means, "Families with children experienced most of the increase in poverty" between 1990 and 1991. Families with children accounted for 1.7 million out of a total increase of 2.1 million (accounting for 80 percent of the poverty increase).[18] In the winter of 1983, for example, CBS aired the docudrama *People Like Us,* which dramatized the life of a young homeless family and challenged many of the stereotypes about homelessness. At the same time, writers were investigating the parameters of this new American poverty. The publication of Ann Marie Rousseau's *Shopping Bag Ladies* and Ellen Baxter and Kim Hopper's *Private Lives, Public Spaces,* along with the harsh winter of 1981–82, "forced [homelessness] to the forefront of public consciousness," according to social historian Michael Katz.[19]

In one sense, the Reagan revolution created a focal point for advocates. In turn, academics, policy experts, and the media noted, with growing concern, the rapidly rising number of poor and homeless Americans. In 1984, Michael Harrington updated his classic *The Other America,* which had introduced President Kennedy to poverty in the early 1960s. In *The New American Poverty,* Harrington called attention to the pervasiveness of poverty in our otherwise-affluent society and suggested that its roots lay deep both in structural impediments to the American dream and in government actions that concentrated on subsidizing the rich and upper middle class rather than eradicating poverty. Harrington blamed neglect and policies protecting the affluent for much of the plight of the poor. He was joined in this attack by other academics and journalists.

In 1983 a group of physicians replicated the 1960 Physician's Task Force study of hunger in America that had served as the basis of Charles Kuralt's CBS documentary *Hunger in America.* Just as that earlier effort increased national concern with poverty in America, the second Physician's Task Force report discussed the resurging prevalence of hunger in America, which, they reported, was overextending emergency support facilities. The Physician's Task Force documented a new type of poverty that included families and children in increasing numbers. Running counter to deeply held beliefs about poverty in America, the new poor lived in families with at least one full-time worker, argued Sar A. Levitan and Issac Shapiro in *Working but Poor.*[20] The emergence of these works reawakened public concern with hunger in America and pointed out that, in the 1980s, poor Americans were increasingly difficult to distinguish from the rest of society. The evidence seemed to suggest that these Americans were as "deserving" as the rest of the country but had become impoverished and in many cases homeless by circumstances beyond their control.

Increasingly the Reagan administration was blamed for growing poverty. Not only did the administration seem to be bullying schoolchildren out of their free lunches, they also seemed to be dealing unfairly by trying to substitute ketchup and pickle relish for vegetables in the school-lunch program.[21] Academics and journalists hinted that government "mean-spiritedness" contributed to the growing poverty rosters and that the White House had been "cooking the books" to hide the actual numbers of poor people. Piven and Cloward made this accusation directly in *The New Class War*, and John Schwarz raised the question in *America's Hidden Success*, as did Harrington in the *New American Poverty*. The Physicians' Task Force published its findings concerning the growing prevalence and threat of hunger in two volumes: *Hunger in America: The Growing Epidemic* in 1983 and *Hunger Reaches Blue Collar America: An Unbalanced Recovery in a Service Economy* in 1987.

The White House countered these accusations by launching the President's Task Force on Hunger in America, which also sent physicians and nutrition experts in search of poverty. Remarkably, the President's Task Force countered the Physicians' Task Force not by suggesting there was no need for emergency support but by arguing that the safety net was intact. The President's Task Force concluded that more money than ever before was being spent to house and feed the poor, proving that the government's response to temporary economic hardship had been sure and swift. The report concluded that problems of poverty were best understood and dealt with at the community level. Therefore, the increasing use of emergency shelters and soup kitchens, far from demonstrating the failure of the Reagan reforms, was proof of their success.[22]

COLLECTIVE ACTION AND POVERTY PROTESTS

Beyond growing academic and journalistic concern, the policy changes and resulting social upheaval of the Reagan reforms increasingly generated street protest, as we saw in the last chapter. These protests, in turn, had the capacity to attract media attention, increase public concern, and gain policy concessions. In return, advocates gained largely symbolic concessions.

Mass mobilization and protest thrust issues into public and political consciousness, lend visibility to the causes represented, and can also lead to the identification of relevant voices, issues, and targets of action. Poor people's advocates protested in response to major national cuts in welfare spending. Advocates took to the streets as Congress debated and adopted cuts in 1981 and 1982. Subsequently, their actions coincided with elections and legislative action, timed to bring poverty and the voice of the poor into policy-making. Protest peaked during congressional elections and when Congress was gearing up to consider major pieces of legislation.

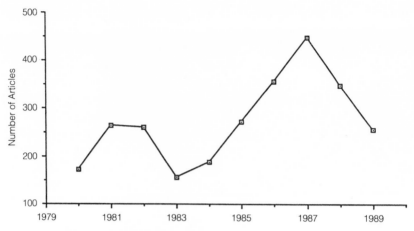

Figure 8: Media Attention to Poverty, by Year, 1980–1989
Source: The New York Times Index

While the protests that attracted media coverage over the decade were concentrated in a handful of larger cities and the nation's capital, they had the capacity to spark much broader national coverage as they were amplified by the media. Advocates adopted made-for-television tactics. They jumped into the Young Republicans' giant cherry pie, disrupted White House tours, and planted rows of corn to feed the poor on the Capitol lawn.

MEDIA ATTENTION: CONSTRUCTING ISSUE SALIENCE

Frank R. Baumgartner and Bryan D. Jones have written, "In the United States, media attention to public policy issues tends to follow a pattern of either feast or famine. Important political questions are often ignored for years, but during certain periods almost every general media outlet features similar stories prominently. Issues are low on the public and media agenda during certain periods, but during others a huge proportion of general media outlets may feature coverage."[23]

During President Reagan's eight years in office, poverty gained extensive attention in the mass media. The *New York Times* printed nearly three thousand articles on poverty in America between 1980 and 1989. From annual data, figure 8 charts the changing level of *New York Times* coverage over the decade. There were two peaks in media attention to poverty over the 1980s. After rising by more than 50 percent between 1980 and 1981, the number of articles in the *New York Times* fell substantially between 1982 and 1983. In 1983, coverage again began to rise, and between 1984 and 1987, levels of media attention to poverty rose steadily. Media attention began to recede in 1988 and 1989 after the adoption of the McKinney Act in 1987, which marked the peak of attention to poverty over the decade.

By examining the aspects of poverty covered by these articles, we gain a sense of the particular facets of poverty as a policy issue that were considered newsworthy. By categorizing each of these three thousand articles according to their principal issue focus, we can discuss the ways in which poverty was presented by the media during this period.

Over the 1980s, the principal aspect of *New York Times* coverage of domestic poverty was the successes, failures, and reallocation debates surrounding existing state and federal welfare programs. The condition and growing numbers of women and children in poverty constituted the second-largest category of text, followed by discussions of the related issues of housing and homelessness. The fourth-largest category concerned the links between poverty and mental illness, particularly in the wake of the deinstitutionalization of mental health patients in the early 1980s.

The high concentration of news stories on government programs and legislative action suggests that one of the critical factors making poverty newsworthy is the frequency and intensity with which it is taken up by state and federal agencies, as well as by Congress and the White House. The ways in which issues are framed and considered by these governing bodies shape the subsequent manner in which the issues are discussed by the press. In this way, media coverage closely follows information provided by and the actions taken by groups within government.[24]

Beyond the *New York Times*, much of the public discussion of poverty in the 1980s furthered the ongoing attempt to categorize who among the poor deserved assistance. It comes as no surprise that the emerging group of poor people considered deserving of assistance over the decade—the homeless—would gain rapidly rising levels of coverage. The *Reader's Guide to Periodical Literature* listed no articles on homelessness in 1975. This number reached thirty-four in 1984 and rose to forty-eight in 1986.[25]

The general trend in attention to poverty over the decade reflects two major shifts in political opportunity. First, corresponding with rising levels of government activity, media attention increased. Between 1982 and 1983, after domestic policy cuts were enacted and federal agendas shifted to other concerns, poverty slipped from the headlines. Reflecting expanding poverty rosters and emerging antipoverty activism from 1983 forward, media attention increased dramatically, peaking with consideration of homelessness legislation in 1987 and dropping off soon thereafter. The picture

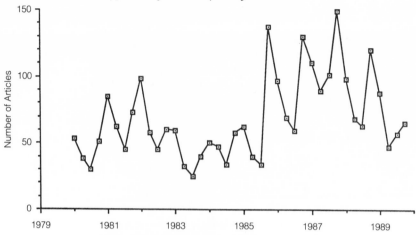

Figure 9: Media Attention to Poverty, by Quarter, 1980–1989
Source: *The New York Times Index.*

becomes much more complex, however, when media attention is disaggregated to quarterly data.

Figure 9 presents a second view of media coverage, charting the number of *New York Times* stories on poverty in three-month segments. By charting total media data in quarter-year increments it is possible to see the effect of seasonal factors on media coverage. The trendline presented in figure 9 shows much more variation in the pattern of attention, indicating strong seasonal variations.

On the average, there were twenty-three articles on domestic poverty in the *New York Times* in each of these 120 months. Deviation from this average, however, was quite large. The year 1983, for example, generated roughly half as much coverage as the decade average, as poverty faded from the public agenda. Conversely, there were 35 percent more stories than average during each month of 1987, corresponding with the debate surrounding consideration and adoption of legislation concerning affordable housing and homelessness.

The dramatically different levels of coverage in winter and summer point to another reality of attention to poverty. The urgency of cold weather shaped both the content and frequency of media coverage. Nearly twice as many stories appeared in December and January (an average of thirty-four) as in July and August (averaging eighteen).

Is there a correlation between protest actions and shifting levels of media coverage? We can offer a tentative measure of the strength of this relation by comparing the number of protests in each quarter-year period with concurrent levels of media coverage. A standard measure of correlation is the Pearson's *r* statistic, which measures the degree to which two sets of events covary. The Pearson's *r* correlation between *New York Times* coverage and levels of protest is a positive 0.35. This relation suggests that levels of protest rose along with levels of media attention to poverty. This relation, however, raises additional questions. First, does protest drive increasing media attention or the reverse? Second, are there other variables (e.g., government action) that cause both media attention and protest to rise?

ISSUE SALIENCE AND PUBLIC OPINION

Rising levels of protest, coupled with increasing press coverage, provided a strong foundation for advocates and activists eager to mobilize general public awareness of hunger and poverty. Did their efforts work? To what extent were Americans concerned with increasing poverty and with government action on poverty over the last decade? Where did Americans place the blame for increasing hunger: on the poor, on state or federal governments, or on general economic conditions? Did rising public concern provide a basis for mobilizing around issues of social justice?

Poverty and welfare continue to evoke conflicting attitudes from the American public. Americans are eager to see that enough is spent on "assistance for the poor," but few support more spending for "welfare." Americans hold firmly to the belief that no one working should be poor, despite the growing numbers of working poor. Where comparable data are available, the American public seems to have been consistently supportive of government antipoverty programs for the last fifty years. In fact, since the New Deal, the American public has consistently told public-opinion pollsters that it supports, at least in broad outline, the notion of public social support.[26]

Between 1981 and 1987, the Gallup polling organization conducted nineteen polls asking Americans to name the most important problem facing the United States. Unemployment and the economy were consistently the most important issues mentioned by respondents, followed by the threat of international tensions and the possibility of war. In these responses we also detect a growing concern with poverty and hunger and with the negative effects of the president's social-services cuts.[27] These results suggest that Americans understood that growing numbers of people were poor and also believed that much of the increase in poverty was due to circumstances beyond the control of the poor themselves.

That the number of Americans living in poverty was rising came as no surprise to most of the country. In 1985, 70 percent of poll respondents said they believed more Americans lived in poverty, despite general prosperity. By August 1989, nearly 83 percent indicated that they believed the number of Americans below the poverty line was increasing.[28]

During the Reagan years, attitudes toward the political dimension of poverty appeared to shift. When asked where responsibility for poverty should be placed, Americans were less certain than at any time since World War II. Over the decade, increasing numbers of Americans blamed poverty on conditions beyond the control of the poor. This change reflects a longer-term shift in American attitudes. In 1964, two-thirds of respondents thought the poor were responsible for their own condition. By the end of the 1980s, 42 percent believed that circumstances beyond individual control accounted for poverty in most cases.[29] This trend continued through the 1980s. Over 70 percent of respondents to a 1989 Gallup poll indicated they were more sympathetic to poor people than they had been five years earlier. This evidence suggests that, over the decade, Americans grew more aware of the complexities surrounding responsibility for poverty and for its alleviation.

We see a similar trend in attitudes toward spending on social-services support. In 1977, 60 percent of respondents held that too much was currently spent on welfare. That percentage dropped over the 1980s (to 47 percent in 1983 and 42 percent in 1988). Toward the end of the Bush administration, only 38 percent of respondents believed too much was spent on welfare. With the transition to the Clinton administration, attitudes seemed to be in transition once again. In 1993, 54 percent of those polled believed too much was spent on welfare—a higher percentage than at any time during the 1980s.[30] This reversal seems to suggest that many Americans equate the Clinton administration's symbolic identification with support for the poor and actual expansions in support.

Still another measure of public concern is found in levels of direct giving. Americans have historically contributed directly to a range of private welfare agencies. Over the 1980s this trend continued. As a percent of gross domestic product, private philanthropy remained steady through the Reagan and Bush administrations. Private philanthropy, however, failed to offset the growing need for support faced by many relief agencies and antipoverty programs. As *Giving USA* reported, "Evidence of increased needs related to poverty apparently did not stimulate a surge in giving to nonprofits addressing those needs. Operators of soup kitchens frequently report that they turn people away because they run out of food, and they stress that donations of food, though essential, cannot replace government grants and private contributions of cash."[31] Commenting on the continuing need for support faced by relief agencies in the early 1990s, the Trust for Philanthropy noted: "Hunger programs and other efforts to assist the poor are still struggling, with a combination of heightened need and declining revenue. While demands for services continue to rise, the value of government contributions continues to erode, and private contributions are modest in relation to the need for funding."[32]

RESPONDING TO RISING ISSUE SALIENCE: CONGRESSIONAL ATTENTION

As poverty gained the attention of the press and led to rising levels of public concern with poverty and homelessness, what responses were elicited from Congress? We can gain a sense of congressional response by looking at the topics considered in the hearing process and the testimony delivered. Congressional hearings provide a forum for airing debates over policy preferences and for constructing consensus around particular options. Hearings offer a useful indicator of how members perceive various policy problems and which representatives of policy preferences are sanctioned.[33] Hearings also provide advocates a relatively low-cost forum to air their concerns, attempt to increase the urgency of their cause, define the terms of debate, and coalesce congressional allies.[34]

The number of hearings Congress holds on an issue provides a useful measure of the degree to which it is considered pressing and deserves symbolic, if not tangible, congressional attention. The *cis Index* of legislative action offers a means to measure congressional attentiveness to poverty by cataloging types of related issues that gained hearings and the total sessions held on poverty-related issues. A general measure of congressional attention to domestic poverty is constructed by combining the number of hearings on budget allocations to welfare programs, child welfare, general nutrition programs, income maintenance, energy assistance, health care and legal aid for the poor, community development programs, unemployment support, homelessness, the elderly poor, and child nutrition (including school lunches).

Figure 10 charts the number of hearings on domestic poverty held by both houses of Congress between 1980 and 1989. As this figure indicates, the number of scheduled hearings on poverty and support for the poor increased steadily across the decade. While fewer than forty poverty and hunger-related hearings were held in 1980, more than 110 were held on the same issues in 1989.

Text from these hearings indicates a number of reasons behind this increase in attention. Hearings early in the decade, for example, considered

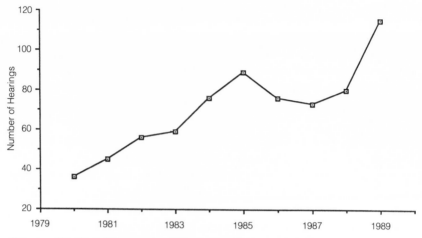

Figure 10: Number of Congressional Hearings on Poverty, 1980–1989
Source: *CIS Index of Subjects & Names, 1980–1990.*

the Reagan budget package and resulted in social-services cuts. Through the middle of the decade, hearings turned increasingly to the issue of hunger in America, responding to a growing number of reports of straining relief services. During the middle of the decade, hunger and poverty became issues on which members of Congress began to air their disagreement with the White House. Toward the end of the decade, more attention was devoted to homelessness in response to growing awareness of this issue and leading to the adoption of the McKinney Act. This shift from the general issue of hunger to much more targeted attention on homelessness suggests that policy agendas gain specificity as they become more urgent. The need to construct an agenda that would gain passage during an era of tight budget constraints meant that many aspects of a poor people's agenda needed to be jettisoned. Thus, during the 1980s, Congress, and increasingly the press and advocates, concentrated on a small number of relatively inexpensive but high-profile, symbolically important programs specifically targeting homelessness, which had come to dominate the national agenda.

SYMBOLIC VERSUS TANGIBLE POLICY RESPONSE

Both insurgent and institutional advocates for the poor shared an overarching objective of securing a sufficient and ongoing federal commitment to alleviating poverty. In many ways, the hearing process is a forum in which Congress offers symbolic concessions to challengers. While hearings bring issues to national attention and allow advocates to voice their concerns, hearings may provide little more than symbolic concessions. In turn, rising levels of congressional action may dissipate advocacy action by offering a level of response to advocates' concerns and demonstrating governmental responsiveness to the issues of poverty and homelessness.

If rising levels of symbolic attention dissipated advocates' action, we would expect to find a negative correlation between the number of scheduled hearings and protest actions over the decade. This inverse relation would suggest that, as congressional attention rises, protest declines. To the contrary, we find a modest and, more important, positive correlation between the number of hearings held and the frequency of protests by antipoverty advocates ($r=0.29$). This positive relation suggests that rising congressional attention to domestic poverty did not dissipate protest action.

A positive association between congressional attention and insurgent advocacy deserves elaboration, however, because hearings serve two purposes: offering an immediate, symbolic response to pressing policy concerns and serving as a preliminary stage in constructing tangible policy decisions, both favorable and unfavorable to advocates. Further, hearings pose another problem. Institutional politics may ultimately diffuse advocates' energies, alienate their own movement base, and dissipate public attention as government appears responsive to their pleas.

Some of the ambiguity of a correlation between insurgency and congressional hearings can be addressed by looking at specific federal policy changes made over the decade. The very act of scheduling hearings may provide a type of symbolic concession to challenging groups without affecting policy outcomes. By turning to indicators of tangible policy change, however, we can gain a more complete sense of the types of policy change that established a context in which collective action was likely to be undertaken by representatives of the poor.

Changes in federal discretionary spending on social services provide a sensitive measure of tangible policy change because discretionary programs (including the social-services block grant, child-welfare services, Head Start, and legal services) are susceptible to annual political attacks.[35] In 1983, Jack Walker noted that the Reagan administration was actively working to frustrate and demobilize their antagonists, including the hunger lobby, through "budget cuts in the discretionary programs of the Great Society."[36] Discretionary programs are politically vulnerable, and we observe shifts in funding to these programs that reflect the political jockeying of the 1980s. As figure 11 indicates, discretionary spending was cut dramatically in 1982. Despite marginal increases in 1984 and 1986, allocations to

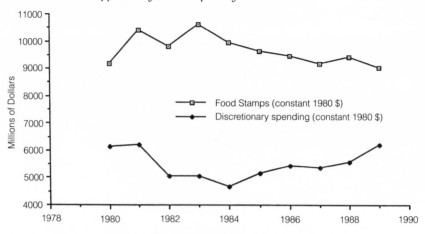

Figure 11: Allocations to Discretionary Programs and Food Stamps, 1980–1989
Source: The Ways and Means Green Book, the Congressional Research Service

discretionary programs remained below 1981 levels during the Reagan presidency.[37] Under the Bush administration, 1981 funding levels were restored, but without expansion.

As we have seen, discretionary program cuts threw the hunger lobby into turmoil. To the extent that discretionary program cuts undermined antipoverty organizations, we might expect to find that cuts in discretionary spending undermined advocates' institutional base and consequently their ability to launch protests. Did discretionary program cuts also dissipate protest actions?

To the contrary, the evidence suggests that there was an inverse relation between protests and changes in discretionary program spending during the 1980s ($r = -0.31$). This negative correlation suggests that, rather than diminish with discretionary program cuts, levels of protest politics rose as federal programs were cut. In other words, advocates protested in response to cuts in discretionary social spending. As this relation indicates, spending cuts, while undermining organized advocacy groups, also heightened the urgency of protest, and insurgent groups responded accordingly. In this sense, spending cuts heightened the urgency and expanded the political opportunity for activism. This relation says two things about protest as a tool of advocates. On the one hand, protest advocacy proved resilient when confronted by one type of adversity. On the other hand, the negative direction of this correlation indicates a principal limitation of protest politics. During periods of program expansion, advocates had a much more difficult time generating protest than during periods of program cuts. This relation suggests that marginal groups in American politics, such as the poor, are much more likely to mobilize in response to threats than to opportunities and that protest politics is more useful for challenging policy threats than for maximizing subsequent incremental victories.

We have seen that cuts in discretionary programs undermined both social services and advocacy organizations. The bulk of antipoverty programs, however, are concentrated within a few entitlement programs, which are much less vulnerable to political attack. Despite the difficulty of cutting entitlement programs, the Reagan administration worked vigorously to cut federal entitlement spending on programs including food stamps, AFDC, and school lunches.

While discretionary program cuts may have left their greatest lasting effect on nonprofit organizations, entitlement cuts directly affected the welfare of millions of Americans. Along with changes in discretionary spending, figure 11 also indicates the annual allocations to the food-stamp program, one of the most widely used social-service programs in this country. The food-stamp program alone draws a much larger share of the budget than the Function 506 discretionary programs already considered. As figure 11 indicates, the appropriation for food stamps faced a series of marginal cuts, which, over the decade, led to a total decline in real terms of 13 percent on the program. Reducing the food-stamp budget during a recession meant fewer services were available to increasing numbers of poor people, who were forced deeper into poverty before qualifying for assistance.

If advocates' attempts to generate protest in support of the poor and homeless were responsive to general changes in social-service spending, we would expect to find a negative correlation between spending on major programs such as food stamps and the number of advocates' actions, which would suggest that cuts in entitlement spending aroused more insurgent activity. As with discretionary programs, we find a robust inverse relation between changes in spending on food stamps and the frequency of antipoverty protests ($r=-0.45$), indicating that protests were much more likely to occur when major entitlement programs such as food stamps were cut. As was the case with discretionary programs, this correlation suggests that, in fact, advocates undertook protest actions in response to major social-policy changes. The negative direction of this correlation again suggests that advocates are much more likely to undertake insurgency actions in response to threats than opportunities.

The relation between protest and social-services spending cuts suggests that insurgent response by weak challengers in the United States is strongly tied to dramatic and threatening policy change. This relation also indicates that, despite retrenchments in avenues for institutional advocacy, advocates still found ways to respond through available venues for action. The highlighted relations also suggest that levels of protest actually increased with levels of symbolic congressional response and that advocates responded to budget cuts in both discretionary and entitlement antipoverty programs.

The combination of attacks on Great Society programs and the increasing salience of poverty and homelessness led advocates to mobilize. When mobilization is constrained in particular directions (e.g., as access to the White House and executive branch agencies was denied to members of the hunger lobby), activists will mobilize in other ways, however tentative. Their actions may include street protest and, potentially, riots. As traditional institutional avenues of access closed, activists adopted more confrontational forms of political expression. For representatives of the poor and homeless, the quest for political voice took them into abandoned buildings, onto the White House grounds, and into the Capitol rotunda. In short, attacks on social-justice programs, coupled with withdrawn institutional access, both constrained institutional action and heightened the urgency of noninstitutional action.

PROTEST AND POLICY CHANGE: WEAK CHALLENGERS
IN AMERICAN DEMOCRACY

Nearly forty years ago, Robert Dahl suggested that groups develop in American politics to represent nascent constituencies, then bargain with political leaders and parties for influence. This chapter has explored the nature of political responses by antipoverty advocates when both their traditional means of political access and traditional allies were unavailable. Advocates responded to constricting operating space with an unlikely and difficult type of political action, taking to the streets in the name of the homeless. Their mobilization offers a potential response to the historical absence of collective identification and action by the poor in this country.

The emergence of this political action suggests that political challenges by the poor and by other weak challenging groups in the United States are much more likely to be *reactionary* than *prospective*. Antipoverty activists took to the streets in reaction to the Reagan agenda. Their protests were undertaken in response to "Reaganomics" in general and to cuts in discretionary and entitlement programs in particular. Cuts in domestic programs were much more likely to elicit protest than were subsequent moves toward expansion. Supporters of the poor did not mobilize to press a general agenda for social reform or to advance a populist candidate. Instead, their protests were geared toward protecting existing social arrangements rather than challenging them.

The relation between the policy process and antipoverty advocacy opens a number of discussions about the conditions under which political mobilization occurs and about the relation among policy change, issue attention, and collective action. Advocates still found a way to mount political actions when mainstream avenues of political access were removed.

For weak challengers such as the poor, collective action proves very difficult to generate and maintain, despite its potential to amplify the voice of the marginalized and powerless. Advocates, however, may adopt the tactics of mass-based movements. The influence of policy change, sectoral upheaval, and issue attention on the emergence of protest suggests that insurgent action occurs in response to factors largely beyond activists' control. In this sense, insurgency may contribute to institutional response, but insurgency itself is usually the product of institutional action.

Ultimately, the Reagan years did not lead to a dramatic expansion in mobilization, but neither did the actions of this administration completely shut down activism. Instead, we see the development of smaller openings for political action. Advocates maintained a foothold in congressional hearings, but they remained a clear minority. Meanwhile, other groups of advocates gained recognition through increasing use of outsider tactics. In confronting less antagonistic regimes, these same strategies and actions will be both more difficult to generate and, paradoxically, more likely to generate preferred policy responses.

Responses to protest, however, range from repression to co-optation to appeasement. In part, responses follow from the interpretation of what groups and issues a particular protest represents, where responsibility for protest is assigned, and how protests are related to the dominant political culture. Further, predicting institutional responses to protest is confounded by the complexity of American federalism. Local, state, and national governments respond differently. Although institutional action precipitates protest, policymakers respond to the extent that insurgency appears to be a coherent reflection of broader societal preferences. Protesting therefore entails uncertainty for advocates. Institutional responses to protest differ and are unpredictable. In this way, even seemingly simple actions may engender a multitude of (more or less apparent) responses.

7

Representing the Poor for
Political Change

One of the ongoing problems with democratic systems concerns citizen involvement in political decision making. Is popular participation the *sine qua non* of a viable democracy? If so, we need to ask who has a voice in decisionmaking and whether existing institutions and practices encourage effective participation.

Social scientists have long noted a number of peculiarities in patterns of participation in democratic societies. Even in the most proudly "classless" societies such as the United States, participation appears to be markedly class based. More affluent citizens are much more likely to be active in politics and are more likely to engage in politics beyond the baseline of voting. Conversely, the least affluent are disproportionately politically apathetic. Analysts point to a number of possible reasons behind this class skew in patterns of participation, including rules of involvement that make it difficult for less mobile, low-income people to become involved, the informal costs of information gathering and participation, the different stakes that low-income and more affluent citizens hold in decision making, and the many factors that make it hard to organize and inform low-income, working Americans. Probably for a combination of all these reasons, poor people collectively are seldom heard in democratic societies around the world, including the United States. This quiescence by the poor is troubling for two reasons. Generally, a systematic underrepresentation of a large and growing group of citizens bodes ill for a society that bases its political identity on the notion of popular sovereignty. Low levels of political involvement by the poor make them easy to ignore. As a result, the poor suffer repeatedly in budget and policy negotiations that take place between representatives of other groups, placing the well being of millions of people on the fringes of security in the hands of those people active in policy networks. Issue networks are filled with representatives of farmers, commodity groups, producers and manufacturers, trade unions, and advocates for competing issues eager to see that larger shares of a shrinking budget are directed toward their own concerns.

Nearly fifteen years ago, Hugh Heclo outlined the ways in which networks of participants surround the making of public policy in the United States.[1] Policy-making, he argued, takes place largely within closely controlled issue networks made up of representatives of bureaucratic agencies, congressional subcommittees, interest groups, and recognized and accepted policy experts. It is difficult for new voices to gain access to long-established policy networks. For new groups to gain access usually requires some jarring external shock announcing an urgent need or glaring oversight.

During the 1980s, a jarring external shock to poverty policy roused advocacy groups for the poor. The extent of their response offers insights into the way direct representation works for the poor. A scattered and tentative outcry did arise from a number of places and groups. We have followed the forms of this resistance and have tried to evaluate how and where it emerged.

The combination of recession, inflation, a growing trade deficit, and domestic tax revolts during the 1970s set the stage for testing the effectiveness of the political infrastructure for poor peoples' representation that had been constructed over the previous two decades. Activist and advocacy groups were positioned, in theory, to mobilize poor and middle-class support for social justice in this country.

Beyond the headlines, poor people's political action draws from a collection of public-interest advocacy groups, bands of activists working within poor communities, and sympathetic academics, journalists, and policy experts. Antipoverty public interest groups cluster in Washington DC, the source of antipoverty policy since the New Deal and Great Society.

National organizations designed to fight poverty developed during the New Deal, but organizations that were specifically concerned with providing political advocacy rather than relief services did not emerge in their present form until the War on Poverty of the 1960s. Critical to their emergence was the shift from local to national responsibility for poverty relief. In addition, through the War on Poverty, the federal government made grant money available for community-action programs, which provided organizational resources where none had existed previously. The 1960s and 1970s were a major period of expansion for antipoverty organizations. Expanding federal grant opportunities allowed for the institutionalization of civil-rights and welfare-rights organizations and encouraged the development of a new entity—the professional antipoverty advocate.

After twenty years of fighting for the poor, poverty advocates were put in the position of also having to fight for their own survival. Two crises faced advocates during the first Reagan term. The combination of economic recession and changing government policies demanded increased social support. At the same time, advocacy groups were threatened by the loss of their major, and, in many cases, only funder.

Depending on government grants rather than mass memberships, these groups appeared immune to the free-rider problem that plagues other public-interest groups. They proved, however, as fragile as other groups when their access to federal funds was removed. Advocates did not fare well in competition with other citizens groups for diminishing private and government grant money. Most poverty advocacy groups were undercut because of their overreliance on a single funding source, which had made them vulnerable to the fallout from ideological shifts between presidential administrations.

While privately funded groups mobilized in response to the Reagan reforms, federally funded groups retrenched. As expected, groups that experience budget crisis have a much more difficult time maintaining consistent organizational and political presence. As Jack Walker indicated in the early 1980s, while presidential administrations will work to further the cause of their allies, they will also work to frustrate their opponents.[2] Under the Reagan administration, social-welfare advocates were squeezed out of traditional avenues of access.

These retrenchments reduced and reconfigured the antipoverty sector. The resulting shifts in representation indicate that stable funding streams to public-interest groups are crucial for maintaining a critical mass of programs and services. In small organizations, whole policy areas may be the responsibility of single individuals. Even small staff reductions may effectively wipe out a group's involvement across a broad range of policy areas. As a result, even small organizational retrenchments often mean fundamentally reshaping programmatic agendas for advocates.

ADVOCATES RESPOND: STRATEGIC ACTION
IN A CONSTRICTING ENVIRONMENT

Advocates adopted two different responses to the recession and political retrenchment of the 1980s. Vestiges of both direct action and representative advocacy were leveled against Congress and the White House. For advocacy groups, political action required finding safe ground on which to approach private and government funders. For activists, resistance required finding a way to enter their own demands into political agendas and overcoming public ignorance and indifference. Although embattled, issue representatives generally managed to survive the 1980s. Their resilience attests to the possibility of direct political involvement by weak groups, suggests that constricting opportunity can sometimes be circumvented, and offers insights into the ways advocates can amplify and potentially ensure the presence of tenuous voices in American politics.

The withdrawal of income posed immediate problems for most advocacy groups. They responded by scrambling to shore up their organizations, stripping management expenditures to the bone, increasing fundraising, and broadening their definitions of political activity to include member services and emergency relief. Meanwhile, private giving increased, to the benefit of some groups, who responded by spending more each year on both organization building (including fund-raising) and on political action. Of necessity, budget needs were primary concerns for these groups. Federal retrenchments made abundantly clear the disadvantages of reliance on a single funder, and advocacy groups took notice and worked to diversify.

Other than fund-raising, strategic responses were predicated on the organizational predicament of individual groups. Hard-hit groups pared back in both size and activity. Where these groups did expand, they did so in directions other than political action. One way to appease members is by increasing specific member services. One group in this study, CNI, largely withdrew from direct lobbying and devoted its energy to producing and distributing its newsletter. Other groups shifted efforts toward providing emergency relief services. One national homelessness advocacy group, for example, found that donors were much more eager to contribute to direct service provision than to political action. In response, the group bought a van and began making rounds of Washington DC streets, delivering coffee, donuts, and blankets to the homeless. Donations to the group increased dramatically.

All these actions have the potential to increase the organizational stability of a group. At the same time, each of these strategies redirect group efforts away from political activity, ostensibly their prime objective. Grantsmanship, member services, and emergency relief provision all divert staff energy and group resources from political action. Admittedly, the payoff for this diversion may be very high and the work performed is urgently needed, but this diversion still means the group is working in a direction other than one originally intended. The alternative for beleaguered groups, however, may be outright retrenchment and substantial cuts in staff, office space, salaries, and issue coverage, again leading to direct reductions in political output.[3]

Groups protected from budget cuts pursued a second set of tactics. With the benefit of organizational security, these public-interest groups adopted new political issues and added new political tactics to their repertoires. A prime example of adding issues is seen in the emergence of Third World famine relief on the agendas of a number of hunger groups as American awareness of the Sahel famine and sympathy with the victims of that emergency grew. New tactics were also adopted as groups worked to sidestep the constraints of institutional politics. These groups had been accepted participants in federal decision making for the previous twenty years. Suddenly outsiders, many groups expanded their tactical arsenal to include street protests and advocacy for specific groups of the deserving poor, such as the homeless, rather than participate in abstract debates over funding levels for nationwide welfare programs. Where market niches were left vacant, new groups formed, sometimes quite successfully. The CBPP, for example, quickly emerged as a leader in congressional lobbying.

Each of these expansionary tactics demanded a level of organizational security to appear rational and viable to group organizers. But the implementation of activist strategies provided another advantage to advocates. Expansionary tactics allowed groups a level of *maneuverability* denied to their retrenching counterparts. By adopting new political issues, for example, advocacy groups were able to frame their agendas to greater advantage. Groups worked to solidify their policy and resource links with their patrons and members as well as with emerging policy concerns. At the same time, they were also able to challenge the agenda control of more powerful actors such as the White House. Likewise, employing new political tactics allowed groups to reevaluate strategic alliances (e.g., with the federal government) and to choose venues and means of access and influence appropriate to a changing political context. Forming new organizations distills the advantages of adopting new issue domains and employing new tactics. Groups that formed during the 1980s escaped the institutional constraints and alliances of older organizations, which were intrinsically linked with federal actions and initiatives, such as the LSC.

These observations suggest that the maneuverability offered by particular tactical choices can be the product of those choices rather than of the relative financial security that made the choices originally appear rational. If this is the case, then a particularly reckless strategy might be rewarded highly. By not adopting the actions of sinking groups, an organization may gain some of the advantages of expanding groups, including name recognition, association with the emerging policy community, a reputation for forceful activism, and consequently the support of potential funders. The FRAC most closely followed this agenda and profited by it in all these ways.

Similarly, advantages come from "biting the hand that feeds" an advocacy group.[4] Increasing confrontation with the federal government will inevitably alienate this funding source, yet when a group is already on the defensive (fending off lawsuits, for example), turning to attack an antagonistic funder may also lead to increased exposure and recognition and potentially to the support of alternative funders. In contrast, political acquiescence may allow a group to ride out periods of antagonism, but at the cost of indefinite periods of political silence, which it may not survive. This point is underscored by the success of those advocacy groups that formed in the breach left beyond the accommodationist tactics and agendas of existing advocacy organizations.

Ultimately, given the unlikelihood that the poor will mobilize directly, political advocacy for social justice may require that organizations in the hunger lobby survive. As resources constricted, groups needed to become more careful and creative fund-raisers, a task made even more difficult by increasing political pressure on tax-exempt organizations supporting unpopular political action. The irs increased its oversight of private foundations, making them more reluctant to invest in political advocacy. Moreover, foundations were simply unequipped to replace the magnitude of funding withdrawn by federal sources.[5] Membership dues and contributions were a second possible source of replacement income. Middle-class Americans, however, remain reluctant to contribute to political advocacy groups, preferring to support direct relief. In general, all economic classes of Americans view political action by the poor with suspicion.[6] Consequently, relief organizations do much better at collecting dues and contributions from a mass base than do their activist counterparts.

Advocacy groups are keenly aware of the funding preferences of the middle class and may shift their focus to emergency relief as a result. Political advocacy suffers in this transferal. As groups turn from politics to service, their remaining political activity increasingly shifts to funding and regulation of the particular services they offer and from political action.[7]

In short, advocacy organizations, as one sector of antipoverty forces, were weakened by reduced budgets and subsequent organizational crisis at the same time they were called on to respond to policy crises. Budget crises limited the effectiveness of public-interest groups as advocates of the disfranchised and limited their ability to encourage the active participation of the poor in politics. By extension, these constraints limit the range of voices in policy-making by reducing the number of representatives for the poor. While a number of criticisms of the interest-group society have been offered, perhaps the most disturbing is that the type of token representation afforded disenfranchised groups by advocacy organizations is not only unlikely to form but is also easily marginalized and quick to fold.

The same set of circumstances that constricted the political opportunity available to institutional advocacy groups also expanded the political opportunity available to more marginalized advocates, who were forced outside institutional channels and into protest. Over the 1980s, the poor and their supporters took to the streets with increasing frequency, gaining media attention, celebrity participation, and agenda space in the process. When compared with more institutionalized interest groups, the expanded media attention given activists suggests that the strategic and tactical options for representatives in this issue sector shifted in response to the increasing constraints governing institutional politics. Issue representatives took advantage of those venues that remained open as well as those that appeared for the first time.

Responding to shifts in political opportunity, activists pressed their demands in new ways. They gained allies, public attention, and media coverage in a much more public and larger political context defined by contemporary political trends, including the emergence of the New Right, the perception of a Republican electoral majority, and the Reagan revolution. Only in this contentious environment could their claims appear critical.

Characteristic of the broader realm of social movements, advocates for the homeless constructed a repertoire of actions appropriate to the types of pressures and context of contention they faced. This collective-action repertoire imported well-known and historically successful types of actions from earlier movements, such as marches, rallies, and sit-ins. Homelessness advocates also were effective innovators, linking homelessness and poverty to broader issues of societal responsibility and political redress. Activists knew developing and implementing creative tactics was critical to keeping homelessness in the news.[8]

Many of these protests attempted to unite groups of poor and homeless people, both to demonstrate their numbers and to link these disparate individuals both symbolically and tangibly. Laura Woliver notes that "groups without ties to a community of memory and hope . . . lack the ideological vision to place their grievances in a social context."[9]

Even setting up a soup kitchen in an unlikely and visible place went far toward fulfilling the objectives of strategists. Because the homeless, like the poor in general, are unlikely to congregate, their number and, therefore, the urgency and legitimacy of homelessness as a political issue are easily diminished. It is much more difficult to dispute the reality of hundreds of people waiting in the cold for a free meal. For the same reason, journalists and conservative analysts who sought to downplay the political significance of these events were keen to discover whether protesters were actually homeless and in need of food or whether they represented a core of liberal agitators or a shiftless group who simply preferred handouts to hard work.

Homeless protests were crafted to link two themes: the misery and danger of life on the street confronting increasing numbers of men, women, and children and the actions and inattention of the Reagan administration that had contributed to the growing numbers of poor people. Tent cities, shantytowns, and soup kitchens made public the grinding poverty and miserable conditions facing homeless people. Actions targeting the White House pointed to the marked disparities in income and opportunity in the United States and the role of government in alleviating hunger and suffering. Chaining themselves to the White House fence and building Reaganville shantytowns, activists linked the president to the homeless. Even more directly, they accused the administration of culpability and neglect, splashing blood on the White House gates and hanging the president in effigy.

By the time *The Nation* declared the homeless movement in full swing in the spring of 1988, mobilization efforts on behalf of the poor and homeless had already made the transition from insider to outsider tactics and back again.[10] The War on Poverty and the Great Society programs established Washington as the center of poverty policy-making. Advocates responded by lobbying Congress and federal agencies for maintained and expanded poverty programs. As public-interest advocates found themselves increasingly pushed outside institutional channels during the 1980s, they embraced guerrilla actions. Following rising public concern with homelessness, the Hands Across America event in May 1986, and passage of the McKinney Act in 1987, advocates were increasingly joined by the public, the media, and government officials. Turnout for demonstrations increased, levels of media coverage rose, and growing agenda space for domestic welfare by the end of the second Reagan term demanded that protesters once again redefine their agendas and actions to retain their effectiveness. In this later incarnation, advocates and activists turned back toward participation in policy networks, undertaking more institutional lobbying and information campaigns.

The Reagan realignment provided a focal point for organizers. Social-justice advocates blamed the administration for domestic poverty and called attention to the rough treatment given the poor by their government, in particular the White House. Similarly, as growing concern with poverty and hunger translated into widening congressional agenda space for action on homelessness, advocates zeroed in on legislative specifics and worked to generate widespread support for full funding of the McKinney Act. Concerned with the fallout of the Reagan agenda, Congress offered legislation to help the poor and homeless. Activists in turn needed to once again respond to agendas determined by other, more powerful actors in the policy-making process. Legislative consideration of the McKinney Act channeled sanctioned actions into a narrower band of acceptable bounds. The peaceful marches and rallies of the late 1980s contrasted with the small acts of civil disobedience and the spate of arrests earlier in the decade. Instead, marches in support of social justice late in the decade much more closely conformed to accepted forms of social protest that had been codified through the civil-rights and antiwar protests of the 1960s. The ultimate example of this "mainstreaming" of social protest was the Hands Across America event in which five million Americans participated nationwide in support of the hungry. The routinized and celebratory nature of this action diffused any vestige of oppositional politics it might have contained. Unlike the direct assaults on the White House of earlier years, this action was nonpartisan and nonaccusatory by design. The fact that this was, in effect, a protest against federal domestic policy was muted to the point that even President and Mrs. Reagan joined the festivities.

Congress was also transformed over the 1980s. With President Reagan's victory, the Republicans gained a majority in the Senate, and the Democrats saw their majority in the House erode. Both chambers, thus reconfigured, adopted policy-making stances shaped by a fear of reprisals against "tax and spend" liberalism and in the shadow of the administration's shifted budget priorities. Under President Reagan's stewardship, Congress adopted a borrow-and-spend ethos that, combined with tax cuts, was offered as a response to the nation's woes.

Over time, congressional Democrats found the fortitude to challenge the president on domestic policy. Several factors contributed to this emerging congressional disagreement with the White House. Critically, the president's electoral coattails failed to carry through the 1982 midterm elections, allowing members to begin to see their electoral security as a separate issue from support for the president. In this climate, Congress slowly rediscovered the domestic economy, made urgent by the recession of 1982. In response to the urgings of cities, states, emergency-service providers, the public-interest community, and the media, congressional hearings were called on domestic conditions, including education, health, and welfare. These congressional deliberations eventually led to a partial reconstruction of a welfare-policy agenda.

Responding to shifting patterns of congressional receptivity, advocates for the poor and homeless also redirected their actions to anticipate and respond to windows of political opportunity as they opened. The tangible opportunities presented by affordable-housing legislation elicited much more focused and specific demands from activists and advocates. Earlier outcries in protest of the administration's "mean spiritedness" were replaced by demands for "full funding of the McKinney Act." In this transformation, issue representatives demonstrated a keen awareness of the opportunities present in the agendas of institutional actors. Early in the decade, widespread support for the administration's domestic welfare cuts led to vague calls by activists for more benevolent behavior. Later, as Congress undertook the process of reinvesting in social services, activists responded with much more specific and targeted demands.

WAS THERE A POOR PEOPLE'S MOVEMENT IN THE 1980S?

The political-process model of movement mobilization posits a number of steps in the emergence of social movements, issue recognition, and political representation. The political representation of the poor over the past decade was marked by vestiges of mobilization, but we are left to conclude these fell short of the threshold of collective behavior constituting a political movement. Movementlike facets of the mobilization include the rising numbers of protest actions and participants in protest events. While poverty protests early in the decade often drew a handful of participants, several of the actions after 1986 included marchers numbering in the thousands. Early in the decade, the means employed by activists were beyond those offered and accepted by mainstream society and resulted in both media exposure and government disavowals and stonewalling.

During this period, poor people's protests were the direct result of the actions of social-movement organizations. Existing advocacy groups able to withstand organizational assault were the first to mobilize. Additionally, new groups formed in the spaces between and alongside existing groups. The revitalization of existing groups and creation of new organizations is a typical pattern of mobilization for movements on the rise.[11]

The revitalization and genesis of social-movement organizations and public-interest groups require that streams of resources flow toward an issue sector. Financial resources, in particular, are made available by concerned patrons, including philanthropists, private foundations, corporate sponsors, celebrities, and government agencies. Their level of interest can take several forms, including donations to the operating funds of movement organizations and participation in movement rallies and protests.

Multiple types of resources were unleashed in the aftermath of the Reagan reforms. While government grant income dropped radically, private contributions rose dramatically. Academic, journalistic, and policy reports on the condition of poor and homeless people appeared with increasing frequency and levels of participation in protest events rose.

Coverage of protests focused on particular groups and individuals as leaders. Increasingly, the media assigned a leadership role to the CCNV and Mitch Snyder. This close association of a particular group with a policy domain grants the organization a tremendous amount of power in defining the agenda of a broader movement.

Just as certain groups become the recognized representatives of their policy domains (e.g., the CDF in the arena of children in poverty), so too are particular activists anointed leaders. Reporters seek out these sanctioned representatives, who become movement celebrities. Snyder, for example, was lionized in a television movie. In turn, other celebrities protested alongside Snyder and CCNV, including Cher, Dr. Benjamin Spock, Philip Berrigan, Jesse Jackson, César Chavez, and members of Congress, including Mickey Leland, Mike Lowry, Joseph P. Kennedy II, and Tony Coelho. Celebrity involvement adds a cachet to protest, legitimates protest actions, and lends them attractive allies. Celebrity also poses a number of dangers, however, diverting attention from activists and dissipating their ability to define the terms of conflict.

THE POLITICAL INFLUENCE OF MOBILIZATIONS FOR THE POOR

The ultimate goal of issue representatives in America remains political accommodation. While activists and advocates entered into broader political dialogue, their influence in these forums was tentative at best. Neither advocates' appeals nor activists' protests stopped budget cuts. Likewise, even though public-opinion polls indicated growing concern with poverty and the effects of the Reagan budget cuts, support for the president remained extremely high, as did suspicions of welfare—suggesting that the public never fully embraced the social-justice movement.

Attempting to carve out an operating platform while skirting the strengths of the president, political activists sought new issues they could control and challenged White House projections on poverty and hunger and its claims to maintaining the safety net protecting the "truly needy." Advocates began to modify their actions to preempt the rhetorical advantage of the administration, for example, in the debate over "hunger in America." Poverty was a more pervasive problem in the United States than hunger and more appropriate to lasting and universalistic government intervention. Nevertheless, the public-interest community concentrated on hunger rather than poverty, allowing activists and advocates to challenge the administration's budget cuts by focusing on the growing number of dire and graphic cases of need.

Concentrating on hunger rather than poverty allowed protesters to emphasize the more dramatic and immediate aspects of their related issues. Their charges were corroborated by reports of growing reliance on shelters and soup kitchens. In this respect, hunger provided a tactical opening that sidestepped the administration's attack on welfare. Still, activists could not have been entirely pleased with this concentration on hunger because emergency relief remains little more than a stopgap measure. In the words of one social-justice advocate, "If you feed the poor, you simply have poor people who are currently fed. The true potential of government is in attacking the structural causes of poverty."[12]

ANTIPOVERTY MOBILIZATION AND POLITICAL OPPORTUNITY STRUCTURES

In democratic systems, a complex interplay of inputs constrains the construction of policy agendas and, therefore, the level of access and influence available to weak challengers. Within the policy process, the inputs of both activists and advocates are bounded by the context in which they operate. Certainly this was true for social-justice advocates over the past decade. Advancing an agenda item in the policy process often follows from some external shock to the political system. These shocks are precipitated by some combination of social upheaval and policy change.

Piven and Cloward have argued that it is possible for the poor to mobilize directly *only* during periods of massive, macrolevel shocks to the political system: "Protest movements do not arise during ordinary periods; they arise when large-scale changes undermine political stability. . . . [E]xtraordinary disturbances in the larger society are required to transform the poor from apathy to hope, from quiescence to indignation. . . . [S]ince periods of profound social dislocations are infrequent, so too are opportunities for protest among the lower classes."[13]

Political interest and concern follows from a major shock to the equilibrium of issue representation as advocates and activists swing into action. Their outcry may capture the attention of the media and raise public awareness of the issue. Increasingly salient issues attract conscience constituents, foundation grants, and alliances with other political groups, policy elites, and concerned individuals. The combined force of these rising resource streams leads to surges of mobilization characterized by widespread public concern and involvement, elite defections from the government's position, and policy change.

While the combination of electoral realignment, policy change, and economic upheaval during the 1980s directly threatened the welfare of lower-class people, these conditions failed to spark the type of direct mobilization Piven and Cloward describe. But the events of the 1980s highlight a second important reality of poor people's representation. Specifically, a poor people's agenda is subsumed within an ongoing policy process that is refined and altered incrementally, often against the current of dominant political rhetoric and public dialogue and with or without the input of a mass mobilization.

In this way, it may be true that periods of political threat are marked both by a failure of the poor to mobilize as well as by the dogged mobilizing efforts of advocates and activists acting on their behalf. A narrowly drawn link between structural upheaval and the agency of protesters has limited utility in that any condition under which protest sputters or fails to develop can be dismissed as structurally inopportune. Yet, as the events of the 1980s suggest, these same periods may generate both street protest and institutional lobbying in the name of the poor and with potential organization, mobilization, and policy consequences.

Entering the 1980s, organized public-interest groups were best positioned to moderate federal retrenchments. Their organizational resources, political experience, connections with members of Congress, and working relations with bureaucratic agencies placed them on the front lines of mobilization efforts. As we have seen, however, they were initially outmaneuvered by the White House. In the early 1980s, advocacy-group program budgets were cut, their allies were diverted by other political battles, and Congress was cowed by tax revolts, the "tax and spend" label, and growing public concern with the budget deficit. In this context, public-interest advocates found themselves battling to maintain their organizations rather than expanding their base of political action.

Cut off from most avenues of institutional action, supporters of the poor pressed their claims in a venue still available to them, protest. As this example suggests, shifts in political opportunity seldom prove to be either wide open or completely shut. Instead, challengers respond to shifting opportunities with what they perceive to be appropriate actions. The degree to which poor Americans can recognize and express their solidarity is severely constrained by structures of social relations and by the nature of American welfare policies, which atomize poor people and dissipate their energies. Moreover, many of the actors active in this issue network, such as the milk lobby and other agricultural commodity groups, are already politically armed and entrenched.

Critical to the mobilization efforts observed was a tangible political assault on concessions won decades ago and now considered assured components of the social contract. Doug McAdam distinguishes between revolutionary and reform goals of social movements.[14] During the 1980s, advocates for the poor were clearly interested in reform rather than revolution. They did not mobilize to press a general agenda for social reform or to advance a populist candidate for office. Instead, their object was less grand and actually reactive rather than prospective. Advocates were intent on protecting rather than challenging social arrangements established through the New Deal and the Great Society program.

One underlying theme of this investigation has centered on the comparative effect of political and economic crisis on advocates and activists for the poor. The same set of events that lead to an organizational crisis can also create a political opportunity for revitalized mobilization. This ambiguity lies at the heart of advocacy representation. Low-level challenges to policy paradigms may be present for years, generating little widespread public concern and few policy concessions. Then, rapidly and with seemingly no change in strategic action, the same set of issue representatives will gain both public and elite attention and support, placing them on the crest of a social movement. Issue representatives and advocacy organizations, in turn, can be swept along the energy of social movements. Advocates are keenly interested in how to trigger this process of mobilization and in harnessing the resources loosened on representatives of salient issues and the political power of social movements.

Where challengers decide to press claims on the political system, they face two types of constraints that both limit and present opportunities.[15] Structures of opportunity are *fixed* when they occur regularly and therefore can be anticipated. For advocates for the poor, fixed aspects of opportunity include regular legislative cycles (in which reallocations for entitlement programs are decided), the annual budget cycle (which sets spending levels on discretionary programs), and the election and work cycles of the House and Senate.

Fixed structures of opportunity provide an annual schedule for activists and advocates. The reallocation cycle of child-nutrition legislation is typical of the ways in which many major social programs are cycled through policy consideration. Facets of child-nutrition programs are reevaluated every three years. Months before hearings are to begin on reallocations to these programs, concerned advocacy groups and think tanks convene workshops and conferences, draw together policy experts and the media, and construct a "causal narrative" that accounts for the strengths and deficiencies of existing programs and offers and negotiates directions for improvement.

Driven by reallocation cycles, this regular, incremental process of policy evolution opens an important window of political opportunity for recognized participants while constraining the potential impact of other, less well recognized or sanctioned voices. Protest undertaken without regard to the window of opportunity may consequently be peripheralized as anomalous and incongruent with broader concerns of the American public. It is much harder to peripheralize actions and issues corroborated by academics, policy experts, and the media. By virtue of this dynamic, agenda space is also opened to activists for marginalized causes, but its form and placement is largely beyond their control. The regularized nature of policy consideration, while initiated by institutional policy networks, also extends opportunities for less powerful voices in the policy-making process. In this respect, activists and advocates peripheral to mainstream politics may *amplify* their own voice by effectively placing their actions within the fray of more entrenched participants who, in effect, open windows of opportunity for themselves as well as for other potential participants.

Variable expansions in political opportunity, on the other hand, are difficult to anticipate and occur only sporadically. Variable policy windows have received much more attention in examinations of social movements and public-interest groups because they are much more dramatic, facilitate explosions of mobilization, and therefore are often thought to be the result of the mobilization process. Variable windows open in response to external shocks to the agenda-setting process, such as when new issues capture political consciousness, seizing public imagination, movement resources, and institutional accommodation, even if only briefly. For social-justice advocates, growing public awareness of a homeless population made otherwise abstract discussions of hunger and poverty graphic. Such issue recognition added an element of dramatic social impact and expanded perceptions of the deserving poor, linking poverty to collective, political response. The consequent introduction of the McKinney Homeless Assistance Act followed logically from this moment of expanding opportunity. In the same way, President Bush's promise of a "kinder, gentler America" responded to increasing public unrest over growing numbers of homeless people, unemployment, and economic frustration.

FINDING OPPORTUNITY IN ADVERSITY

The development of a social-movement cycle is beyond the control and largely beyond the influence of individual groups. The aspects of political context that create both fixed and variable policy windows, however, can often be anticipated and, in this sense, provide opportunities for activists.

While such structures may constrain, they also define space to maneuver. Advocates both seek ways to maximize their influence within the confines available to them and inevitably test the limits of those confines. Consequently, insurgent actions, if well placed, can anticipate the next opening of a policy window. As the examples in this work have suggested, the relation between challenging groups and levels of political opportunity remains in flux.

Where actions are launched against rigid structures of opportunity, they are much less likely to elicit desired responses. The effects of unfavorable placement can be disheartening. Participants in protest events, for example, often bristle when media accounts are used to measure levels of insurgency, because many actions that were important to their participants are never discussed in the national press. In a very real sense, however, these actions failed to become part of the lasting record of insurgency.

Windows of opportunity both open and close for activists. Actions taken during closed periods are much less likely to gain coverage than those undertaken in the context of legislative action, which draws media concern. In this respect, activists will be peripheralized when they fail to acknowledge the constraints of opportunity structures. Conversely, they can also gain amplification by placing their activities within emerging structural openings.

The difference between events that occur during openings in political opportunity and those that fall between the cracks can be the difference between attention and inattention to policy positions. This may also account for the difference between claims that simmer at low levels for long periods of time and those which boil over into widespread mobilization.

The actions of recognized insider groups, both institutional and extra-institutional, contribute formally to policy agendas and contribute much to the scheduling of debate and action. An example of this tendency is seen in the CCNV, which became a regular participant in congressional hearings. Likewise, as public-interest advocates scramble to shape the record created through allocation hearings, they interact with other groups in a political context largely beyond their control. Setting and manipulating legislative cycles are strategic acts undertaken by particular, sanctioned, institutional actors that influence the actions not only of other insider groups but also of less well recognized and less institutional groups and individuals.

As a result, the actions of well-positioned advocates establish opportunities both for themselves and for other weaker and peripheral actors in the policy process. Anticipating recurring aspects of policy, advocates augment scheduled activities with their own events, designed to attract thoughtful contributions, focused debate, and widespread attention. Street protest becomes codified into month-long "calls to civil disobedience," for example, with coordinated actions, a regularly briefed media, and advance arrangements with the police for transporting those arrested. To the extent these actors are successful, their actions increase the policy opening not only for their own position but also for the interests and concerns of even more marginalized groups. In this way, media reports of a new study of the pervasiveness of homelessness establish an attentiveness to this issue that translates into a search for political dimensions of the issue, that is, heightening interest in homeless protests. While think tanks and established advocacy groups construct facets of the larger agenda for their own purposes, the opening they force is available to dissidents, challengers, and insurgents operating at the fringes of institutional politics.

In this respect, protests well placed relative to other policy agendas can advantage both their reception and their contribution to political dialogues. Activists, therefore, can amplify the impact of their actions not simply through tactical choice but also through placement of their actions. Various public-interest groups, social-movement organizations, private foundations, corporations, elected officials, bureau representatives, and concerned individuals will have different but compounding influences on the construction of policy.

The roles available to marginalized challengers depend on their starting point relative to centers of decision making. The example of social-justice advocacy in the 1980s offers a corollary to this observation. Organized public-interest groups will do what they are positioned to do—push for institutional recognition, ask government agents to intercede on their behalf, and call for public involvement. In all these ways, the organized mobilize.

At the same time, rising concern with a constituency or policy position will lead to the organization and mobilization of the previously unmobilized. Direct political action by activist organizations for homeless Americans, as well as marches and rallies demanding that government act on homelessness, brought forth new political groups and new participants in political action. In response to rising national awareness of growing poverty and homeless rosters, new public-interest groups and social-movement organizations formed in a period of severe resource contraction.

Notes

INTRODUCTION

1. Schattschneider 1960.

2. Verba et al. 1993:303–18.

3. This section owes much to the insights shared by professors Jo Freeman, Andy McFarland, David Meyer, and Robert Salisbury.

CHAPTER ONE: REAGAN AND THE POOR

1. Ford Foundation, *Annual Report,* 1989:11–12; Macchiarola and Gartner 1989:21; Phillips 1990.

2. Patterson 1986.

3. Weber 1990.

4. U.S. Bureau of the Census, Current Population Reports 1991. Series P-60, No. 181, "Poverty in the United States," and Special Tabulations; U.S. House Committee on Ways and Means 1993:1308, 1309, 1311, 1315; Rodgers:1986.

5. Tarrow 1994a:188.

6. Meyer 1990:2.

7. Meyer 1990:5.

8. McAdam 1982:21.

9. Freeman 1983:195–96.

10. Freeman 1983:197.

11. Freeman 1983:208.

12. Freeman 1983:23.

13. Freeman 1983:199.

14. Woliver 1993.

15. Evans and Boyte 1992:17–18.

16. Beckwith 1992; Fantasia 1988; Freeman 1983.

17. Freeman 1983:9.

18. Freeman 1983:26.

19. McAdam 1982:44–46.

20. Zald and Ash 1987; Freeman 1983; Marwell and Oliver 1993.

21. Piven and Cloward 1979.

22. McAdam 1982:27; Emery and Trist 1973; Wilson 1973.

23. Freeman 1983.

24. Freeman 1983.

25. McCarthy and Zald 1987; Salisbury 1989.

26. McAdam 1982.

27. Tarrow 1991.

28. Meyer and Imig 1993.

29. Fisher 1993.

30. Tarrow 1994a:85–86.

31. Eisinger 1973.

32. McAdam 1982:170.

33. Freeman 1975; Jenkins and Perrow 1977; Lipsky 1970; Meyer 1990; Piven and Cloward 1979.

34. Gamson and Meyer, n.d.; McAdam 1982; Meyer and Imig 1993.

35. Meyer 1990.

36. Lipsky 1970; Jenkins and Perrow 1977; Piven and Cloward 1979.

37. McAdam 1982:49; Meyer 1990:11.

38. Hamilton et. al. 1948.

39. Hamilton et. al. 1948.

40. Dahl 1956; Garson 1978; Truman 1951.

41. McConnell 1967; Schattschneider 1960; Schlozman 1984:1014; Schlozman and Tierney 1986; Walker 1983, 1991; Wilson 1973.

42. Verba and Nie 1972.

43. Gamson 1990.

44. Hacker 1991; Hochschild 1981.

45. Kieweit 1983.

46. Kieweit 1983; Piven and Cloward 1979; Pope 1989.

47. Schlozman and Verba 1979:240.

48. Schlozman and Verba 1979:240.

49. Hochschild 1981.

50. Schlozman and Tierney 1986.

51. Berry 1977.

52. McAdam 1982; Verba and Nie 1972: chap. 10.

53. Pope 1989:51–54.

54. Pope 1989:51.

55. Pope 1989:52–53.

56. Edsall and Edsall 1991.

57. Goldfield 1987.

58. Piven and Cloward 1979:72; Schlozman and Verba 1979:339.

59. Sousa 1992.

CHAPTER TWO: THE REAGAN REVOLUTION IN DOMESTIC SPENDING

1. U.S. House Committee on Ways and Means 1993:1367.

2. McAdam 1982:43.

3. Katz 1989.

4. Children's Defense Fund 1994:2; U.S. House Committee on Ways and Means 1993:1313.

5. Levitan and Shapiro 1987. The authors discuss the American conviction that one can climb out of poverty through diligence and hard work. Among their findings, about six million poor people in 1985 lived in familes with at least one full-time, year-round worker yet with a family income below the poverty line. At the same time, public-opinion data strongly suggest Americans believe that no family with a full-time worker will be poor.

6. The poverty line is equivalent to three times the cost of the "thrifty food plan," which constitutes a minimally adequate diet. The figure is based on national spending trends in the 1950s, when the average low-income family spent one third of its income on food and roughly the same percentage on housing (including utilities). Today, housing costs amount to more than half of the average poor family's income. See Ruggles 1990:A12.

7. Anderson 1988:109–39; Meyer 1990; Palmer and Sawhill 1982:23.

8. Palmer and Sawhill 1982:14.

9. Anderson 1988; Boskin 1989; Stockman 1987.

10. A July 1894 study by the Congressional Research Service indicated that the enactment of OBRA increased the number of persons in poverty in 1982 by 2 percent over the number that would have been classified as poor had the 1981 AFDC program gone unchanged. In addition, the weak economy increased the number of poor Americans by nearly 6 percent. When combined with the impact of OBRA, the economy operated to increase the number of the poor by almost 8 percent, or one person in twelve. The number of individuals below the poverty level increased by 8.5 million from 1975 to 1982; U.S. House Committee on the Budget 1984:268.

11. U.S. House Committee on Ways and Means 1993:1367.

12. Nathan, Doolittle, and associates 1987:44–66; *CQ Almanac* 1981:461.

13. Gillon 1992:302.

14. Gillon 1992:302.

15. Gillon 1992:310; Greider 1982.

16. Quoted in Phillips 1990:74.

17. Although not all of the administration's proposed reductions in child-nutrition programs were enacted, program expenditures were reduced by 28 percent ($5.15 billion) between 1982 and 1985. Food Research and Action Center 1990; National School Boards Association, n.d.

18. U.S. House Committee on the Budget 1984:253; Burtless 1992:26–29.

19. Lazere et. al. 1994.

20. Jencks 1994b:42.

21. Center on Budget and Policy Priorities 1988.

22. *CQ Almanac* 1983:413–14.

23. Brown and Pizer 1987:224–25.

24. *CQ Almanac* 1981:91, 463.

25. Melnick 1994:80.

26. *CQ Almanac* 1981:466.

27. These conclusions of the U.S. Conference of Mayors report, as well as Representative Panetta's remarks concerning the increased use of feeding centers, are found in the 1983 *CQ Almanac*:413–14.

28. *CQ Almanac* 1983:413.

29. *CQ Almanac* 1983:413–14.

30. *CQ Almanac* 1983:413.

31. *CQ Almanac* 1983:415.

32. *CQ Almanac* 1983:437.

33. *CQ Almanac* 1984:139.

34. *CQ Almanac* 1985:525.

35. *CQ Almanac* 1988:187.

36. Phillips 1990.

37. Phillips 1990:210.

38. Cutler and Katz 1992:41.

39. Physicians' Task Force on Hunger in America 1987:6.

40. Blustein 1988:A8; Physicians' Task Force 1987:5, chap. 3; Schwarz 1988; Katz 1989:242; Greenstein 1989.

41. Kenworthy 1991.

42. U.S. House Committee on Ways and Means 1993:1405; Rich 1990.

43. Rich 1990.

44. Wilson 1992.

45. For a related discussion, see Schneider 1992:33–44.

CHAPTER THREE: THE HISTORICAL DEVELOPMENT OF
POVERTY ADVOCACY

1. Allen 1994: C1; Weaver 1994:18–21.

2. Leiby 1978:193.

3. Katz 1983:5.

4. Katz 1989.

5. Kutzner 1993; Lammers 1982:138.

6. Katz 1983:41.

7. Katz 1983:6.

8. Moynihan 1969:34.

9. See, for example, Gutman 1976; Rodgers 1978; Thernstrom 1964.

10. Domhoff 1990; Jenkins and Brents 1989:891–909; Quadagno 1988.

11. Katz 1983:9.

12. Leiby 1978:170.

13. President's Research Committee on Social Trends 1933:1202ff.

14. Lanning 1981; Lubove 1965; Leiby 1978; Smith 1987:12.

15. Moynihan 1969:35.

16. Ylvisaker is quoted in Moynihan 1969:36.

17. Bradbury 1962; Katz 1983:8.

18. Leuchtenburg 1963:118–42.

19. Heclo 1986:314.

20. Skocpol 1992.

21. Leuchtenburg 1963:338.

22. Leiby 1978:300.

23. Lemann 1988; Nathan, Doolittle, and associates 1987: chap. 4.

24. Lemann 1988.

25. Lemann 1988.

26. Haverman 1988:18–19.

27. The emphasis on services rather than structural problems marked the War on Poverty from the beginning: "Although the most influential analyses of poverty stressed its roots in unemployment, federal antipoverty planners deliberately avoided programs that created jobs. . . . Despite its structural diagnosis, the Council of Economic Advisors laid the foundation for a War on Poverty based on economic growth, civil rights, and new social and educational services designed to equalize opportunity. The council stressed removing the handicaps that denied the poor 'fair access to the expanding incomes of a growing economy.'" Katz 1989:91–92.

28. The relation between the War on Poverty and the civil-rights movement is discussed in Allen 1969; Katz 1989.

29. Lemann 1994.

30. Zarefsky 1986:43–44.

31. Office of Economic Opportunity, n.d.:A7.

32. Davis 1993; Freeman 1983; West 1981.

33. Schlozman and Tierney 1986:130–31; Wilson 1973:46–47.

34. Leiby 1978:337.

35. This section is based on interviews with former staff members of the Emergency Food and Medical Services Program, the Community Food and Nutrition Program (CFNP), and the original grantees of these agencies, including FRAC and CNI.

36. The CFNP was the congressional response to the Citizen's Board of Inquiry Into Hunger and Malnutrition and its publication, *Hunger U.S.A.* The Citizen's Board of Inquiry was financed by the Marshall Field Foundation to investigate the extent of hunger in America. Results of this investigation were heard by Congress in considering the OEO Act of 1964.

37. Davis 1993; author's interviews.

38. Lemann 1989:63.

39. Melnick 1994:80.

40. Lemann 1989:63. The author goes on to note, "That unpleasant period in the past that Republicans like to talk about, when we threw money at our problems, was really the first Nixon Administration more than it was either of the Democratic administrations of the sixties."

41. Nathan, Doolittle, and associates 1987:39.

42. Lemann 1989:68.

43. Nathan, Doolittle, and associates 1987:42; Phillips 1990:64.

44. Author's interviews; Lammers 1982:141.

45. Hansen 1991; Hayes 1983:112–16.

46. In 1981, 6,600 groups maintained Washington offices. By 1989 this number had nearly doubled; Close 1989; Loomis and Cigler 1983.

47. Schlozman and Tierney 1986:10–11.

48. McConnell 1967:3.

49. Tocqueville 1966.

50. Bentley [1908] 1967.

51. Madison, Hamilton, and Jay 1966.

52. Hofstadter 1955:225–54.

53. Heclo 1979.

54. Garson 1978:77.

55. Truman 1951:138.

56. Wootton 1985:1.

57. "Ideological" or public-interest groups have been around in some form since the founding of the nation. An example of a successful early public-interest groups is the Anti-Saloon League, founded in 1832 (see Odegard 1928). A number of other venerable public-interest groups, such as the Sierra Club and John Muir Society, remain active today.

58. Loomis and Cigler 1983:1–2; McFarland 1984.

59. Abuses of the term *public interest* are apparent even in this example, since producers of synthetic fibers or promoters of the use of other animal furs may benefit

from the proposed ban while claiming to support it in the interest of the seal's well-being (see Yandle 1984). Yandle finds throughout history an intertwining of selective and material interests in much successful lobbying on regulatory policy; see also Berry 1977: chap. 1.

60. Chong 1991; Olson 1971.

61. Walker 1983:394. Government subsidies to private political actors are not new. One of the best-known examples of federal support for interest advocacy is the American Farm Bureau Federation (AFBF). Established by the Smith-Lever Act of 1914, the AFBF historically provided both a political voice for rural farmers and an information network through which Congress could assess the needs of farmers and inform the public about congressional action. The AFBF quickly adopted an active role in policy-making: writing legislation, gathering information, and participating in budgeting decisions. In turn, the group's lobbying efforts increased both the stature of and appropriations to the Department of Agriculture.

62. Schlozman and Tierney 1986:59–87.

63. Berry 1977:9. "Organizations that receive their funding from government sources, such as some legal aid or community action groups, which might otherwise qualify as public interest, are not considered within the scope of the definition [of public-interest groups]. Groups supported by the government operate under a much different set of constraints."

64. Walker 1983:397–98. Public-interest groups draw funds from more *types* of funding sources than either trade associations or unions. The total number of their contributors, however, remains much smaller.

65. Emery and Trist 1973.

66. Walker 1983:397.

67. Ford Foundation 1989: xiii.

68. Ford Foundation 1982: v.

69. Keller 1981:659–64.

70. Keller 1981:664.

71. For a discussion of inflation rates between 1980 and 1985, see Nathan, Doolittle, and associates 1987: chap. 3; Greenstein 1989. For foundation responses to increased funding requests from poverty advocates, see Keller 1981:664.

72. Schnaue 1982:62–63.

73. Peterson and Walker 1986:168.

74. Smith and Lipsky 1993; Walker 1983.

75. Peterson and Walker 1986:168.

CHAPTER FOUR: PUBLIC-INTEREST-GROUP RESPONSES

1. An earlier version of several of these arguments appeared in Imig 1992.

2. "'The Reagan Administration . . . Watt, . . . Gorsuch and company—are fan-

tastic fund raisers for [the Sierra Club],' said John McComb, director of the club's Washington office"; Stanfield 1981:1378.

3. Salisbury 1984; Schlozman and Tierney 1986.

4. This list is compiled from multiple sources, including the *Encyclopedia of Associations*, lists of participants in congressional hearings (e.g., the CIS *Index*), media accounts of protest events, and the author's interviews. The *Encyclopedia of Associations* is a comprehensive directory of American organizations, which provides fundamental information about their missions, budgets, memberships, and founding dates. The directory includes listings for antipoverty groups, as well as those concerned with homelessness, children's welfare, and community action. The *Encyclopedia of Associations* can be augmented with media accounts and information gathered in interviews.

This list is not exhaustive. Organizations exclusively providing services are not included. The Beef Cattle Drive for Hunger, for example, is a national antihunger group formed by the Lady Cattlemen's Association with the mission of donating vouchers for beef to the poor. Groups that focus on direct services (including the Beef Cattle Drive for Hunger) are passed over because they avoid political action. Similarly, a large number of familiar church groups balance a small percentage of advocacy with a primary concern with providing emergency relief; Schlozman 1984; Walker 1983.

5. See Woliver 1993 for a discussion of the importance of these links to an organization's success.

6. Peterson and Walker 1986:166.

7. Peterson and Walker 1986:171.

8. Peterson and Walker 1986:166.

9. Kutzner 1993:90.

10. Author's interviews, Interfaith Hunger Appeal, 1990.

11. Author's interviews, 1989–94.

12. Author's interviews, CBPP, 1990.

13. Quoted in Stanfield 1981:1376.

14. Internal Revenue Service 990 forms are filed by tax-exempt organizations and reveal financial characteristics of public-interest groups, including yearly funding levels, sources of income, and programmatic spending.

15. Testimony delivery, while ambiguously related to political effectiveness, is a common measure of political activity both for academics and for interest groups. Schlozman and Tierney 1986 (e.g., 295).

16. Some analysts look to regional organizations and service providers for political mobilization and policy change. Given the pervasive need for emergency relief in this country, these organizations might provide a nationwide infrastructure for political action (see Hoehn 1993). At the same time, the institutional constraints on

these same groups make their activism more difficult and less likely to crystalize (see Mullins 1986:7–8).

17. Center on Social Welfare Policy and Law, n.d.

18. Davis 1993.

19. Melnick 1994.

20. Gale Research 1985.

21. Gale Research 1990.

22. Kutzner 1993:90.

23. Bread for the World *Annual Report* 1982.

24. Founded in 1940 by Marshall Field III, the Field Foundation provided support to the cbpp, frac, cdf, the Center for Defense Information, and the Study Group on Social Security before spending itself out of existence in 1989.

25. Author's interview, cbpp, 1990.

26. Gale Research 1990.

27. Imig 1994.

28. Schlozman and Tierney 1986:91.

29. Peterson and Walker 1986:175.

30. All financial information and all trend computations are reported in or based on constant 1980 dollars.

31. Smith and Lipsky 1993.

32. Although income and spending patterns of these groups fluctuated annually, comparing 1981 to 1985 establishes the parameters of group mobilization during the first Reagan term. Comparisons with 1988 allow us to identify continuing changes over the second Reagan term.

33. Author's interviews, cswpl, 1989–93.

34. Author's interviews, frac, 1990.

35. The cni lost many of its institutional records from this period because of a fire and reorganization, according to a group representative. This overview is reconstructed from audited financial statements and irs 990 forms.

36. Serio and Company 1985:1.

37. Author's interviews, bfw, 1990.

38. Staff members offer this assessment on the basis of the type of direct-mail appeals that elicited memberships, contributions, member comments, and letters (author's interview).

39. Hopkins 1987:268–80. Tax-exempt political activity may include nonpartisan analysis and research for elected officials, responding to written requests from governmental officials with technical advice or help, and meeting and communicating with legislators about effects of their decisions on the organization's existence.

40. Measures of testimony delivery were constructed from listings in 1976 through 1986 editions of the *Congressional Information Service Annual Index*.

41. Author's interview, FRAC, 1990.

42. Author's interview, FRAC, 1990.

43. Author's interviews, CNI, 1990, 1994.

44. Author's interview, BFW, 1990.

45. Author's interview, BFW, 1990.

46. Author's interview, BFW, 1990.

47. Author's interview, BFW, 1990.

48. Author's interview, BFW, 1990.

49. Author's interview, BFW, 1990.

50. Author's interview, CBPP, 1991.

51. Author's interview, FRAC, 1990.

52. Author's interview, FRAC, 1990.

53. Author's interviews, BFW, 1990. Group sensitivity to member wishes have been noted for other public-interest groups (see McFarland 1984).

54. Sabatier 1992.

55. See Leonard and Greenstein 1994.

56. Dahl 1956.

57. Eisinger 1973; Tilly 1978.

58. Emery and Trist 1973:148.

59. Wilson 1973:31.

CHAPTER FIVE: POLITICS BY OTHER MEANS

1. McAdam 1982:57–58.

2. McAdam 1982:58.

3. Author's interviews, CCNV, 1994.

4. In this respect, the homeless movement was more like the environmental movement than the civil-rights or women's movements (Costain 1992:3).

5. Meyer 1990:2.

6. Piven and Cloward 1979:36.

7. Yates and Kinoy 1991.

8. Piven and Cloward 1979:12.

9. Tilly 1986:3.

10. Gurr 1970; Hoffer 1951; Kornhauser 1959.

11. Lipsky 1970.

12. Tarrow 1991:15.

13. Rochon 1988:109.

14. Beckwith 1992.

15. Beckwith 1992:13.

16. Fantasia 1988:25–74; Goldfield 1987; Piven and Cloward 1979.

17. Fantasia 1988:227.

18. Rochon 1988:109.

19. Imig and Meyer 1993; Jenkins and Perrow 1977; McAdam 1982; Meyer 1990.

20. To compile this information, I made use of an electronic media archive, the *Nexis Omni File*. This archive is an information service comprising an on-line full-text database containing an extensive collection of national newspapers, including the *New York Times, Washington Post, Chicago Tribune,* and *Los Angeles Times*. In addition, *Nexis* includes transcripts from daily television newscasts and reports filed by a number of wire services, including the United Press International, PR Newswire, and States News Service. The electronic nature of this medium allows researchers to search for particular topics on the basis of key words, greatly reducing the time involved in full-text events data searches.

21. Author's interviews, CCNV, 1994.

22. Stanfield, 1994:532–36.

23. *CQ Almanac* 1987:508.

24. This chronology is limited to the media accounts presented in the *Nexis Omni File*. Consequently, the account has a large-city bias, where large-circulation papers are found. Further, the data overlook all instances that did not gain media coverage. This bias conforms to the research agenda of this book to the extent that media attention is fundamental to generating or constructing a level of "issue attention." For this reason, I make the assumption that coverage in one of the national newspapers or wire services provides a useful baseline of issue attention. The usefulness of the data set also depends on the keywords searched. Exploratory runs using subject headings from the Library of Congress, *Encyclopedia of Associations,* and *Washington Representatives* addressed this problem. Working from news collections required combining multiple discussions of singular events. In this way, events were counted only once, and multiple sources allowed for compiling details. This method made it possible to follow the buildup for a march or demonstration as well as its aftermath. This data source also allowed for analysis of several nonevents, including protests that were scheduled but never took place. In several examples, concessions were elicited *before* actions were held. In one interpretation, concessions preempted protest. In another, concessions attest to the power of the insurgents and their proposed action.

25. To minimize the confusion caused when multiple issues are raised, I include only actions undertaken principally and explicitly for the homeless.

26. To posit that issues are not simply reported but are "framed" suggests that a number of largely true narratives can be offered to explain most policy issues. Only a few of these narratives, however, will be told. The process of choosing which stories to tell and the victims and culprits in these stories and linking the action to other social issues and movements follows from explanations offered by advocates and institutional actors. As Laura Woliver notes, issue construction and framing are central to the

experiences of challenging groups and movements. A social-movement affiliation, for example, may provide groups with the language and political stance needed to make sense of their issues and sustain their group momentum; Woliver 1993:166.

27. Woliver 1993:55.

28. Peterson and Walker 1986.

29. Author's interviews, Homes Not Jails, 1994.

30. United Press International, 24 October 1982.

31. United Press International, 24 October 1982.

32. United Press International, 3 August 1982; *Los Angeles Times,* 3 July 1986.

33. *New York Times,* 2 December 1981.

34. United Press International, 25 October 1982.

35. McCarthy, McPhail, and Smith 1992.

36. *New York Times,* 27 October 1984, 4 November 1984, 28 February 1986; United Press International, 15 February 1986; *Los Angeles Times,* 28 February 1986.

37. *Newsweek,* 24 December 1984.

38. *Christian Science Monitor,* 21 September 1986.

39. *Christian Science Monitor,* 21 September 1986.

40. *New York Times,* 19 August 1983.

41. United Press International, 2 August 1984.

42. United Press International, 15 September 1984.

43. *New York Times,* 27 October 1984.

44. Author's interviews, CCNV, 1994.

45. *National Journal,* 15 December 1984; *New York Times,* 5 November 1984. Over the fifty-one-day fast, Snyder lost more than sixty pounds (*New York Times,* 10 November 1984).

46. Author's interviews, CCNV, 1994.

47. United Press International, 3 August 1982.

48. *Washington Post,* 25 January 1983.

49. United Press International, 26 May 1986.

50. Reuters, 4 May 1987.

51. States News Service, 2 November 1988.

52. States News Service, 13 October 1988.

53. Author's interviews, CCNV, 1994.

54. States News Service, 1 October 1988.

55. States News Service, 13 October 1988.

56. United Press International, 21 October 1988.

57. States News Service, 2 November 1988.

58. States News Service, 2 November 1988.

59. PR Newswire, 4 November 1988.

60. Author's interviews, CCNV, Homes Not Jails, 1994; *CQ Almanac* 1987:507.

61. States News Service, 2 November 1988.

62. Kessler 1988.

63. United Press International, 25 October 1982.

64. *New York Times*, 8 November 1988.

65. United Press International, 29 April 1989.

66. *Los Angeles Times*, 30 April 1989.

67. *Los Angeles Times*, 8 October 1989.

68. Yates and Kinoy 1991.

69. *Los Angeles Times*, 8 October 1989.

70. McAdam 1982:176.

71. Woliver 1993.

72. Holsworth 1989:138.

73. Holsworth 1989.

74. Epstein 1991.

75. *New York Times*, 8 November 1988; *States News Service*, 2 November 1988.

76. Beckwith 1992; McAdam 1982.

77. *Washington Post*, 26 January 1983.

78. *New York Times*, 8 November 1988.

79. McAdam 1982; Pope 1989.

80. Pope 1989:137.

81. Kessler 1988.

82. Hobsbawm 1959:172–74.

83. In any case, they argue, organizations at best work to exploit the potential influence of poor people's protest when institutional conditions are favorable; Piven and Cloward 1979:37.

84. United Press International, 19 January 1985.

85. United Press International, 19 June 1986.

86. Kessler 1988.

87. *Nexis Omni File* 1994. *Textline News Service.*

CHAPTER SIX: POLITICAL OPPORTUNITY AND ANTIPOVERTY ACTIVISM

1. Greider 1982.

2. Costain 1992; McAdam 1982; Tarrow 1991.

3. Meyer and Imig 1993:253–70.

4. Tarrow 1991.

5. Downs 1972; Kingdon 1984.

6. Heclo 1979:87–124.

7. Hansen 1991.

8. Kingdon 1984.

9. Lehmann 1988, 1989; Stone 1989:281.

10. Gitlin 1980.

11. Piven and Cloward 1979:273.

12. McCarthy and Zald 1987.

13. Moynihan 1969.

14. Greenstein 1985:12–17.

15. Brown and Pizer 1987.

16. Stone 1989:281–300.

17. Salisbury 1989:28.

18. U.S. House Committee on Ways and Means 1993:1308.

19. Katz 1989:193.

20. Levitan and Shapiro 1987.

21. Food Research and Action Center 1990.

22. President's Task Force on Food Assistance 1984.

23. Baumgartner and Jones 1993:20.

24. Entman 1989.

25. Katz 1989:192.

26. Erikson, Luttbeg, and Tedin 1988:56–59.

27. To construct a measure covering this period, I combine two comparable questions concerning the Reagan budget cuts and growing concern with hunger and poverty into a single indicator.

28. *Gallup Reporter*, 10–13 August 1989:5.

29. *Gallup Reporter*, 10–13 August 1989:7.

30. Barnes 1994:516–20.

31. American Association for Responsible Charity 1993:139.

32. American Association for Responsible Charity 1993:139.

33. Hansen 1991.

34. According to Schlozman and Tierney (1986:295), "Testifying at Congressional hearings . . . is the most widely used [interest group] technique of influence. What is more, Washington representatives . . . deemed it an important activity: 27 percent mentioned testifying at hearings as one of the three activities . . . which consume the most time and resources."

35. Abramson and Salamon 1986:118.

36. Walker 1983:404.

37. These programs make up function 506 of the federal budget. They include the social-services block grant, child-welfare services, foster care, community-services block grant, rehabilitation services, social-services other groups, Head Start, social services for the elderly, domestic volunteers, housing counseling assistance, other social services, criminal-justice assistance, legal services, and family services. (Another study using these programs as a proxy for discretionary spending on social welfare may be found in Abramson and Salamon 1986:118).

CHAPTER SEVEN: REPRESENTING THE POOR FOR POLITICAL CHANGE

1. Heclo 1979:87–124.

2. Walker 1983.

3. Holsworth 1989.

4. Pope 1989.

5. *CQ Weekly Report*, 18 April 1981:663.

6. Lipsky 1970.

7. Smith and Lipsky 1993.

8. Author's interviews, CCNV, 1994.

9. Woliver 1993:166.

10. *The Nation*, 16 April 1988.

11. Tarrow 1991.

12. Author's interviews, 1990.

13. Piven and Cloward 1979: 14, 28.

14. McAdam 1982:58.

15. A similar argument is made by Gamson and Meyer (n.d.).

Bibliography

Abramson, Alan J., and Lester M. Salamon. 1986. *The Nonprofit Sector and the New Federal Budget*. Washington DC: Urban Institute.

Allen, Jodi. 1994. "Welfare Terminator II: How Clinton Can End Reform as We've Known It," *Washington Post*, 19 June, C1.

Allen, Robert L. 1969. *Black Awakening in Capitalist America: An Analytic History*. Garden City NY: Doubleday.

Amenta, Edwin, et al. 1987. "The Political Origins of Unemployment Insurance in Five American States." *Studies in American Political Development* 2:137–82.

American Association for Responsible Charity. 1980–94. *Giving USA*. New York: AAFRC Trust for Philanthropy.

Anderson, Martin. 1988. *Revolution*. New York: Harcourt Brace Jovanovich.

Bacharach, Peter, and Morton Baratz. 1970. *Power and Poverty: Theory and Practice*. New York: Oxford University Press.

Barnes, James A. 1994. "Waiting for Clinton." *National Journal*, 5 March, 516–20.

Bassuk, Ellen L. 1991. "Homeless Families." *Scientific American*, December, 66–71.

Baumgartner, Frank R., and Bryan D. Jones. 1993. *Agendas and Instability in American Politics*. Chicago: University of Chicago Press.

Baxter, Ellen, and Kim Hopper. 1981. *Private Lives/Public Spaces: Homeless Adults on the Streets of New York City*. New York: Institute for Social Welfare Research.

Beckwith, Karen. 1992. "Collective Action and Action Repertoires in the 1989–1990 UMW Strike against Pittston Coal Group." Paper presented at the NEH Summer Seminar on Political Histories of Collective Action, Ithaca NY.

Bentley, Arthur F. [1908] 1967. *The Process of Government*. Cambridge MA: Harvard University Press.

Berry, Jeffrey. 1977. *Lobbying for the People*. Princeton NJ: Princeton University Press.

———. 1984a. *Feeding Hungry People: Rulemaking in the Food Stamp Program*. New Brunswick NJ: Rutgers University Press.

———. 1984b. *The Interest Group Society*. Boston: Little, Brown.

Blustein, Paul. 1988. "Peace for All, Prosperity—for Some." *Washington Post National Weekly Edition*, 3–9 October, A8.

Boskin, Michael A. 1989. *Reagan and the Economy: The Successes, Failures and Unfinished Agenda*. San Francisco: ICS.

Bradbury, Dorothy E. 1962. *Five Decades of Action for Children: A History of the Children's Bureau*. Washington DC: Government Printing Office.

Bread for the World. 1982. *Annual Report*. Washington DC: Bread for the World.

Brown, J. Larry, and H. F. Pizer. 1987. *Living Hungry in America*. New York: Macmillan.

Burt, Martha R. 1992. *Over the Edge: The Growth of Homelessness in the 1980s*. New York: Russell Sage Foundation and Urban Institute Press.

Burtless, Gary. 1992. "When Work Doesn't Work: Employment Programs for Welfare Recipients." *Brookings Review*, Spring: 26–29.

Center on Budget and Policy Priorities. 1988. *Analysis of Changes in Food Stamp Participation*. Washington DC: Center on Budget and Policy Priorities.

Children's Defense Fund. 1994. *The State of America's Children: Yearbook 1994*. Washington DC: Children's Defense Fund.

Center on Social Welfare Policy and Law. n.d. "A Description of the Center on Social Welfare Policy and Law." New York: Center on Social Welfare Policy and Law.

Chong, Dennis. 1991. *Collective Action and the Civil Rights Movement*. Chicago: University of Chicago Press.

Close, Arthur C. (ed.). 1981–1990. *Washington Representatives*. Washington DC: Columbia.

Congressional Information Service. 1976–1986. *CIS Annual Index*. Bethesda MD: Congressional Information Service.

Cook, Faye Lomax, and Edith J. Barrett. 1992. *Support for the American Welfare State*. New York: Columbia University Press.

Costain, Anne. 1992. *Inviting Women's Rebellion*. Baltimore: Johns Hopkins University Press.

CQ Almanac. 1980–1992. Washington DC: Congressional Quarterly Press.

Cutler, David M., and Lawrence F. Katz. 1992. "Untouched by the Rising Tide: Why the 1980s Economic Expansion Left the Poor Behind." *Brookings Review*, Winter: 40–46.

Dahl, Robert. 1956. *A Preface to Democratic Theory*. Chicago: University of Chicago Press.

Danziger, Sheldon H., and Daniel H. Weinberg. 1986. *Fighting Poverty: What Works and What Doesn't*. Cambridge MA: Harvard University Press.

Davis, Martha F. 1993. *Brutal Need: Lawyers and the Welfare Rights Movement, 1960–1970*. New Haven CT: Yale University Press.

Demkopich, Linda E. 1984. "Traffic Cop, Troubleshooters and True Believers." *National Journal*, 15 December, 2411.

Domhoff, William G. 1990. *The Power Elite and the State: How Policy Is Made in America*. New York: de Gruyter.

Downs, Anthony. 1972. "Up and Down with Ecology: The Issue-Attention Cycle." *Public Interest* 28 (Summer): 38–50.

Edsall, Thomas Byrne, and Mary D. Edsall. 1991. *Chain Reaction: The Impact of Race, Rights and Taxes on American Politics*. New York: Norton.

Eisinger, Peter. 1973. "The Conditions of Protest Behavior in American Cities." *American Political Science Review* 67:11–28.

Ellwood, John (ed.). 1982. *Reductions in U.S.Domestic Spending*. New Brunswick NJ: Transaction.

Emery, F. E., and E. L. Trist. 1973. "The Causal Texture of Organizational Environments." In *Tomorrow's Organizations: Challenges and Strategies*, Jong S. Jun and William B. Storm, eds., 141–51. Glenview IL: Scott, Foresman.

Entman, Robert. 1989. *Democracy without Citizens: Media and the Decay of American Politics*. New York: Oxford University Press.

Epstein, Barbara. 1991. *Political Protest and Cultural Revolution: Nonviolent Direct Action in the 1970s and 1980s*. Berkeley and Los Angeles: University of California Press.

Erikson, Robert S., Norman R. Luttbeg, and Kent L. Tedin. 1988. *American Public Opinion: Its Origins, Content and Impact*. 3d ed. New York: Macmillian.

Evans, Sara M., and Harry C. Boyte. 1992. *Free Spaces: The Sources of Democratic Change in America*. Chicago: University of Chicago.

Fantasia, Rick. 1988. *Cultures of Solidarity: Consciousness, Action and Contemporary American Workers*. Berkeley and Los Angeles: University of California Press.

Fisher, Stephen L. (ed.). 1993. *Fighting Back in Appalachia: Traditions of Resistance and Change*. Philadelphia: Temple University Press.

Food Research and Action Center. 1990. *20 Years: Food Research and Action Center*. Washington DC: Food Research and Action Center.

Ford Foundation. 1980–1993. *Annual Reports*. New York: Ford Foundation.

Freeman, Jo. 1975. *The Politics of Women's Liberation*. New York: McKay.

———. 1983. *Social Movements of the Sixties and Seventies*. New York: Longman.

Gale Research. 1980–94. *Encyclopedia of Associations*. Detroit: Gale Research.

Gallop Poll. *The Gallup Report*. 10–13 August 1989.

Gamson, William A. 1990. *The Strategy of Social Protest*. Belmont CA: Wadsworth.

Gamson, William A., and David S. Meyer. n.d. "Framing Political Opportunity." In *Opportunities, Mobilizing Structures and Framing: Comparative Applications of Contemporary Movement Theory*, Doug McAdam et al., eds.(forthcoming).

Garson, G. David. 1974. "On the Origins of Interest-Group Theory: A Critique of a Process." *American Political Science Review* 68 (December): 1505–19.

———. 1978. *Groups Theories of Politics*. Beverly Hills CA: Sage.

Gaventa, John. 1981. *Power and Powerlessness: Quiescence and Rebellion in an Appalachian Valley*. Urbana: University of Illinois Press.

Gillon, Steven M. 1992. *The Democrats' Dilemma: Walter F. Mondale and the Liberal Legacy*. New York: Columbia University Press.

Gitlin, Todd. 1980. *The Whole World Is Watching: Mass Media in the Making and Unmaking of the New Left*. Berkeley: University of California Press.

Goldfield, Michael. 1987. *The Decline of Organized Labor in the United States*. Chicago: University of Chicago Press.

Greenstein, Robert. 1985. "Losing Faith in *Losing Ground*." *New Republic,* 25 March, 12–17.

———. 1989. *Increased Poverty and Growing Inequality: What the 101st Congress Can Do*. Washington DC: Center on Budget and Policy Priorities.

Greider, William. 1982. *The Education of David Stockman and Other Americans*. New York: Dutton.

Gurr, Ted Robert. 1970. *Why Men Rebel*. Princeton NJ: Princeton University Press.

Gutman, Herbert G. 1976. *Work, Culture, and Society in Industrializing America*. New York: Knopf.

Hacker, Andrew. 1991. "Class Dismissed." *New York Review of Books,* 7 March, 44–47.

Hamilton, Alexander, et al. 1948. *The Federalist Papers*. New York: Penguin.

Hansen, John Mark. 1987. "Choosing Sides: The Creation of an Agricultural Policy Network in Congress, 1919–1932." In *Studies in American Political Development*, 2d ed., 183–229.

———. 1991. *Gaining Access: Congress and the Farm Lobby, 1919–1981*. Chicago: University of Chicago Press.

Harrington, Michael. 1970. *The Other America*. New York: Macmillan.

———. 1985. *The New American Poverty*. New York: Penguin.

Haverman, Robert. 1988. *Starting Even: An Equal Opportunity Program to Combat the Nation's New Poverty*. New York: Simon & Schuster.

Hayes, Michael T. 1983. "Interest Groups: Pluralism or Mass Society?" In *Interest Group Politics*. Washington DC: Congressional Quarterly Press.

Heclo, Hugh. 1979. "Issue Networks and the Executive Establishment." In *The New American Political System*, Anthony King, ed. Washington DC: American Enterprise Institute for Public Policy Research.

Hertzke, Allen. 1988. *Representing God in Washington*. Knoxville: University of Tennessee Press.

Hobsbawm, Eric. 1959. *Primitive Rebels: Studies in Archaic Forms of Social Movement in the 19th and 20th Centuries*. Manchester: Manchester University Press.

Hochschild, Jennifer. 1981. *What's Fair? American Beliefs about Distributive Justice.* Cambridge MA: Harvard University Press.

Hoehn, Richard A. 1993. "The U.S. Feeding Movement—Fertile Ground for an Anti-Hunger Movement." In *Hunger 1994: Transforming the Politics of Hunger,* 11–19. Silver Spring MD: Bread for the World Institute.

Hoffer, Eric. 1951. *The True Believer.* New York: Harper & Row.

Hofstadter, Richard. 1955. *The Age of Reform.* New York: Knopf.

Holsworth, Robert D. 1989. *Let Your Life Speak: A Study of Politics, Religion, and Antinuclear Weapons Activism.* Madison: University of Wisconsin Press.

Hopkins, Bruce R. 1987. *The Law of Tax Exempt Organizations.* 5th ed. New York: Wiley.

Imig, Douglas. 1992. "Resource Mobilization and Survival Tactics of Poverty Advocacy Groups." *Western Political Quarterly* 45(2): 501–20.

———. 1993. "Mobilization of the Hunger Lobby: Issue Attention, Collective Action and Institutional Response." Paper presented at the 1992 annual meeting of the American Political Science Association, Chicago.

———. 1994. "Presidential Administrations and Political Opportunity." Paper presented at the 1994 annual meeting of the Midwest Political Science Association, Chicago.

Imig, Douglas, and David Meyer. 1993. "Political Opportunity and Peace and Justice Advocacy in the 1980s: A Tale of Two Sectors." *Social Science Quarterly* 74(4): 750–70.

Iyengar, Shanto. 1991. *Is Anyone Responsible? How Television Frames Political Issues.* Chicago: University of Chicago Press.

Jenkins, J. Craig, and Barbara G. Brents. 1989. "Social Protest, Hegemonic Competition, and Social Reform: A Political Struggle Interpretation of the Origins of the American Welfare State." *American Sociological Review* 54: 891–909.

Jenkins, J. Craig, and Charles Perrow. 1977. "Insurgency of the Powerless: Farm Worker Movements 1946–1972." *American Sociological Review* 42:249–68.

Jencks, Christopher. 1994a. *The Homeless.* Cambridge MA: Harvard University Press.

Jencks, Christopher. 1994b. "Housing the Homeless." *New York Review of Books,* 12 May, 39–45.

Jun, Jong S., and William B. Storm (eds.). 1973. *Tomorrow's Organizations: Challenges and Strategies.* Glenview IL: Scott, Foresman.

Katz, Michael. 1983. *Poverty and Policy in American History.* New York: Academic Press.

———. 1989. *The Undeserving Poor.* New York: Pantheon.

Keller, Bill. 1981. "Facing the Reagan Ax: Special Treatment No Longer Given Advocates for the Poor." *Congressional Quarterly Weekly Reports,* 18 April, 659–64.

Kenworthy, Tom. 1991. "15 Years of Cuts Said to Enrich the Rich." *Washington Post*, 13 September, A23.

Kessler, Brad. 1988. "The Homeless Movement: After Charity, Start Organizing." *The Nation*, 16 April, 528–30.

Kieweit, D. Roderick. 1983. *Macroeconomics and Micropolitics*. Chicago: University of Chicago Press.

Kingdon, John. 1984. *Agendas, Alternatives and Public Policies*. Boston: Little, Brown.

Kornhauser, William. 1959. *The Politics of Mass Society*. Glencoe IL: Free Press.

Kutzner, Patricia L. 1993. "Thirty Years of Anti-hunger Advocacy." In *Hunger 1994: Transforming the Politics of Hunger*, 83–98. Silver Spring MD: Bread for the World Institute.

Lammers, Nancy (ed.) 1982. *The Washington Lobby*. Washington DC: Congressional Quarterly Press.

Lanning, Hugh. 1981. *Government and Voluntary Sector in the USA*. London: National Council for Voluntary Organizations.

Lazere, Edward, Paul Leonard, Cushing Dolbeare, and Barry Zigas. 1994. *A Place to Call Home: The Low Income Housing Crisis Continues*. Washington DC: Center on Budget and Policy Priorities and Low Income Housing Information Service.

Lemann, Nicholas. 1988–1989. "The Unfinished War," pts. 1–2. *Atlantic Monthly*, December and January.

———. 1994. "How Not to Fight Poverty." *New York Times Magazine*, 9 January, 27–60.

Leiby, James. 1978. *A History of Social Welfare and Social Work in the United States*. New York: Columbia University Press.

Leonard, Paul A., and Robert Greenstein. 1994. *Life Under the Spending Cap: The Clinton Fiscal Year 1995 Budget*. Washington DC: Center on Budget and Policy Priorities.

Leuchtenburg, William E. 1963. *Franklin D. Roosevelt and the New Deal, 1932–1940*. New York: Harper & Row.

Levitan, Sar A., and Isaac Shapiro. 1987. *Working but Poor: America's Contradiction*. Baltimore: Johns Hopkins University Press.

Lipsky, Michael. 1970. *Protest in City Politics: Rent Strikes, Housing and the Power of the Poor*. Chicago: Rand McNally.

Loomis, Burdett A., and Allan J. Cigler (eds.). 1983. *Interest Group Politics*. Washington DC: Congressional Quarterly Press.

Lowi, Theodore. 1979. *The End of Liberalism*. New York: Norton.

Lubove, Roy. 1965. *The Professional Altruist*. New York: Athenaeum.

Macchiarola, Frank J., and Alan Gartner (eds.). 1989. *Caring for America's Children*. New York Academy of Political Science.

Madison, James, Alexander Hamilton, and John Jay. 1966. *The Federalist Papers: A*

Collection of Essays Written in Support of the Constitution of the United States, Roy P. Fairfield, ed. Garden City: Anchor Books.

Marwell, Gerald, and Pam Oliver. 1993. *The Critical Mass in Collective Action: A Microsocial Theory*. New York: Cambridge University Press.

McAdam, Doug. 1982. *Political Process and the Development of Black Insurgency*. Chicago: University of Chicago Press.

———. 1988. *Freedom Summer*. New York: Oxford University Press.

McAdam, Doug, John McCarthy, and Mayer Zald (eds.). Forthcoming. *Opportunities, Mobilizing Structures and Framing Processes*. New York: Cambridge University Press.

McCarthy, John D., Clark McPhail, and Jackie Smith. 1992. "The Tip of the Iceberg: Some Dimensions of Selection Bias in Media Coverage of Demonstrations in Washington, D.C., 1982." Paper delivered at the annual meeting of the American Sociological Association, Pittsburgh, 21 August.

McCarthy, John D., and Meyer N. Zald. 1987. "Resource Mobilization and Social Movements: A Partial Theory." In *Social Movements in an Organizational Society*, Meyer Zald and John D. McCarthy, eds. New Brunswick NJ: Transaction.

McConnell, Grant. 1967. *Private Power and American Democracy*. New York: Knopf.

McFarland, Andrew S. 1984. *Common Cause: Lobbying in the Public Interest*. Chatham NJ: Chatham House.

———. 1993. *Cooperative Pluralism: The National Coal Policy Experiment*. Lawrence: University Press of Kansas.

Melnick, R. Shep. 1994. *Between the Lines: Interpreting Welfare Rights*. Washington DC: Brookings Institute Press.

Meyer, David S. 1990. *A Winter of Discontent: The Nuclear Freeze and American Politics*. New York: Praeger.

Meyer, David S., and Doug Imig. 1993. "Political Opportunity and the Rise and Decline of Interest Group Sectors." *Social Science Journal* 30:253–71.

Mills, C. Wright. 1956. *The Power Elite*. New York: Oxford University Press.

Moe, Terry M. 1980. *The Organization of Interests*. Chicago: Rand McNally.

———. 1981. "Toward a Broader View of Interest Groups." *Journal of Politics* 43:531–45.

Moynihan, Daniel P. 1969. *Maximum Feasible Misunderstanding: Community Action in the War on Poverty*. New York: Free Press.

Mullins, Phil. 1986. "The Name of the Game Is Power." *The Neighborhood Works*, May, 7–8.

Nathan, Richard P., Fred C. Doolittle, and associates. 1987. *Reagan and the States*. Princeton NJ: Princeton University Press.

National Commission on Excellence in Education. 1983. *A Nation at Risk: The Imperative for Educational Reform. A Report to the Nation and the Secretary of Education,*

United States Department of Education. Washington DC: Commission on Excellence in Education.

National School Boards Association. n.d. *National School Boards Association School Lunch Survey*. Alexandria VA: National School Boards Association.

Odegard, Peter H. 1928. *Pressure Politics, the Story of the Anti-Saloon League*. New York: Columbia University Press.

Olson, Mancur. 1971. *The Logic of Collective Action*. Cambridge MA: Harvard University Press.

Office of Economic Opportunity. n.d. *Community Action Workbook*. Washington DC: Office of Economic Opportunity.

Palmer, John, and Isabel Sawhill (eds.). 1982. *The Reagan Experiment: An Examination of Economic and Social Policies under the Reagan Administration*. Washington DC: Urban Institute.

———. (eds.). 1984. *The Reagan Record: An Assessment of America's Changing Domestic Priorities*. Cambridge MA: Ballinger.

Patterson, James T. 1986. *America's Struggle against Poverty, 1900–1985*. Cambridge MA: Harvard University Press.

Peterson, Mark A., and Jack L. Walker. 1986. "Interest Group Responses to Partisan Change." In *Interest Group Politics*, Allan J. Cigler and Burdett A. Loomis, eds., 2d ed. Washington DC: Congressional Quarterly Press.

———. 1991. "Interest Groups and the Reagan Presidency." In *Mobilizing Interest Groups in America*, Jack L. Walker, ed. Ann Arbor: University of Michigan Press.

Petracca, Mark P. (ed.). 1992. *The Politics of Interests: Interest Groups Transformed*. Boulder CO: Westview.

Phillips, Kevin. 1990. *The Politics of Rich and Poor*. New York: Random House.

———. 1992. *Boiling Point*. New York: Random House.

Physicians' Task Force on Hunger in America. 1987. *Hunger Reaches Blue Collar America: An Unbalanced Recovery in a Service Economy*. Cambridge MA: Harvard University Press.

Piven, Francis Fox, and Richard A. Cloward. 1979. *Poor People's Movements: Why They Succeed, How They Fail*. New York: Vintage.

———. 1982. *The New Class War*. New York: Pantheon.

Pope, Jacqueline. 1989. *Biting the Hand That Feeds Them: Organizing Women on Welfare at the Grass Roots Level*. New York: Praeger.

President's Research Committee on Social Trends. 1933. *Recent Social Trends in the United States*. New York: McGraw Hill.

President's Task Force on Food Assistance. 1984. *Report of the President's Task Force on Food Assistance*. Washington DC: President's Task Force.

Quadagno, Jill S. 1988. *The Transformation of Old Age Security: Class and Politics in the American Welfare State*. Chicago: University of Chicago Press.

Rich, Spencer. 1990. "Capital Gains and the Widening Income Gap." *Washington Post*, 24 July, A21–A24.

———. 1992. "The Rich Got Richer, Again: The Gap Widens between Haves and Have-Nots." *Washington Post National Weekly Edition*, 14–20 September, 37.

Rochon, Thomas R. 1988. *Mobilizing for Peace: The Antinuclear Movements in Western Europe*. Princeton NJ: Princeton University.

Rodgers, Daniel T. 1978. *The Work Ethic in Industrial America, 1850–1920*. Chicago: University of Chicago Press.

Rodgers, Harrell R. 1986. *Poor Women, Poor Families: The Economic Plight of America's Female-Headed Households*. Armonk NY: Sharpe.

Rossi, Peter H. 1989. *Down and Out in America: The Origins of Homelessness*. Chicago: University of Chicago Press.

———. 1993. "The Politics of Homelessness." In *Sociology and the Public Agenda*, William Julius Wilson, ed., 287–99. Newbury Park CA: Sage.

Rothenberg, Lawrence S. 1992. *Linking Citizens to Government: Interest Group Politics at Common Cause*. New York: Cambridge University Press.

Rousseau, Ann Marie. 1981. *Shopping Bag Ladies: Homeless Women Speak about Their Lives*. New York: Pilgrim.

Ruggles, Patricia. 1990. "The Poverty Line: Too Low for the 90s." *New York Times*, 26 April, A12.

Sabatier, Paul A. 1992. "Interest Group Membership and Organization: Multiple Theories." In *The Politics of Interests*, Mark Petracca, ed., 99–129. Boulder CO: Westview.

Salamon, Lester, and Alan J. Abramson. 1991. "The Federal Budget and the Nonprofit Sector: FY 1992." Occasional Paper No. 9, Johns Hopkins University Institute for Policy Studies, Baltimore.

Salisbury, Robert. 1969. "An Exchange Theory of Interest Groups." *Midwest Journal of Political Science* 13(1): 1–32.

———. 1984. "Interest Representation: The Dominance of Institutions." *American Political Science Review* 78:64–76.

———. 1989. "Political Movements in American Politics: An Essay on Concept and Analysis." In *New Perspectives in American Politics*, Lucius Barker, ed., 15–30. New Brunswick NJ: Transaction.

Schattschneider, E. E. 1960. *The Semi-sovereign People*. New York: Holt, Reinhart & Wilson.

Schlozman, Kay Lehman. 1984. "What Accent the Heavenly Chorus? Political Equality and the American Pressure System." *Journal of Politics* 46:1006–32.

Schlozman, Kay L., and John Tierney. 1986. *Organized Interests and American Democracy*. New York: Harper & Row.

Schlozman, Kay L., and Sidney Verba. 1979. *Injury to Insult: Unemployment, Class and Political Response*. Cambridge MA: Harvard University Press.

Schneider, Anne, and Helen Ingram. 1993. "Social Construction of Target Populations: Implications for Politics and Policy." *American Political Science Review* 82(7): 334–47.

Schneider, William. 1992. "The Suburban Century Begins." *Atlantic Monthly*, July, 33–44.

Schwarz, John E. 1988. *America's Hidden Success: A Reassessment of Public Policy from Kennedy to Reagan*. New York: Norton.

Schwarz, John E., and Thomas J. Volgy. 1992. *The Forgotten Americans*. New York: Norton.

Serio and Company. 1985. *Community Nutrition Institute, Audited Financial Statement* (September 10). Washington DC: Serio & Company.

Skocpol, Theda. 1992. *Protecting Soldiers and Mothers: The Political Origins of Social Policy in the United States*. Cambridge MA: Harvard University Press.

Smith, Steven Rathgeb. 1987. "Government, Nonprofit Agencies and the Welfare State." Ph.D diss., Department of Political Science, Massachusetts Institute of Technology.

Smith, Steven Rathgeb, and Michael Lipsky. 1993. *The Age of Contracting*. Cambridge MA: Harvard University Press.

Sousa, David. 1992. "Union Decline and American Politics." Paper presented at the annual meeting of the American Political Science Association.

Stanfield, Rochelle L. 1981. "'Defunding the Left' May Remain Just Another Fond Dream of Conservatives." *National Journal*, 1 August, 1374–78.

———. 1994. "The Dispossessed." *National Journal*, 5 March, 532–36.

Stockman, David A. 1987. *The Triumph of Politics*. New York: Avon.

Stone, Deborah A. 1989. "Causal Stories and the Formation of Policy Agendas." *Political Science Quarterly* 104(2): 281–300.

Tarrow, Sidney. 1991. *Struggle, Politics and Reform: Collective Action, Social Movements and Cycles of Protest*. Ithaca NY: Cornell Center for International Studies.

———. 1994a. *Power in Movement: Social Movements, Collective Action and Politics*. New York: Cambridge University Press.

———. 1994b. "Social and Political Movements." *Enciclopedia della Scienze Sociali*. Rome: Institute della Enciclopedia Italiana.

Thernstrom, Stephen. 1964. *Poverty and Progress: Social Mobility in a Nineteenth-Century City*. Cambridge MA: Harvard University Press.

Tilly, Charles. 1978. *From Mobilization to Revolution*. Reading MA: Addison-Wesley.

———. 1986. *The Contentious French*. Cambridge MA: Harvard University Press.

Tocqueville, Alexis de. 1966. *Democracy in America*. Medford MA: Tufts University Press.

Truman, David B. 1951. *The Governmental Process*. New York: Knopf.

U.S. House Committee on the Budget. 1984. *A Review of President Reagan's Budget Recommendations, 1981–1985*. Washington DC: Government Printing Office.

U.S. House Committee on Ways and Means. 1993. *Green Book: Background Material and Data on Programs within the Jurisdiction of the Committee on Ways and Means*. Washington DC: Government Printing Office.

Verba, Sidney, and Norman H. Nie. 1972. *Participation in America: Political Democracy and Social Equality*. Chicago: University of Chicago Press.

Verba, Sidney, Kay Lehman Schlozman, Henry Brady, and Norman H. Nie. 1993. "Citizen Activity: Who Participates? What Do They Say?" *American Political Science Review* 87(2): 303–18.

Walker, Jack L. 1983. "The Origin and Maintenance of Interest Groups in America." *American Political Science Review* 72(2): 390–406.

———. 1991. *Mobilizing Interest Groups in America: Patrons, Professions, and Social Movements*. Ann Arbor: University of Michigan Press.

Weaver, Kent. 1994. "Old Traps, New Twists: Why Welfare Is So Hard to Reform in 1994." *Brookings Review* 12(3): 18–21.

West, Guida. 1981. *The National Welfare Rights Movement: The Social Protest of Poor Women*. New York: Praeger.

Wilson, James Q. 1973. *Political Organizations*. New York: Basic Books.

———. 1990. "Malaise II." *Commentary*, October, 54–56.

Wilson, James Q. 1992. "To Prevent Riots, Reduce Black Crime." *The Wall Street Journal*, 6 May, A16.

Woliver, Laura. 1993. *From Outrage to Action*. Urbana: University of Illinois Press.

Wootton, Graham. 1985. *Interest Groups: Policy and Politics in America*. Englewood Cliffs NJ: Prentice-Hall.

Yandle, Bruce. 1984. "Intertwined Interests, Rent Seeking and Regulation." *Social Sciences Quarterly* 65: 1002–12.

Yates, Pamela, and Peter Kinoy. 1991. *Takeover*. New York: Skylight Pictures.

Zald, Meyer, and Roberta Ash. 1987. "Social Movement Organizations: Growth, Decay, and Change." In *Social Movements in an Organizational Society*, Meyer Zald and Roberta Ash, eds., 121–41. New Brunswick NJ: Transaction.

Zald, Meyer, and John D. McCarthy. 1987. *Social Movements in an Organizational Society*. New Brunswick NJ: Transaction.

Zarefsky, David. 1986. *President Johnson's War on Poverty: Rhetoric and History*. Tuscaloosa: University of Alabama Press.

Index

DATE DUE

ILL: 6259932		
SJD: 8/5/97		
Due: 9/4/97		
DEC 2 3 1998		
DEC 2 2 1999		